To SAM
Pray for Revival
Elmer Tow...
9-25-22

REVIVAL
IGNITERS

Other Destiny Image Books by Elmer L. Towns

The Bible by Jesus

Faith to Plant Churches

Planting Reproducing Churches

Prayer Journey Bible

Praying Paul's Letters

Praying the Book of Revelation

Praying the New Testament

Praying the Heart of David

Praying for Your Children (with David Earley)

How God Answers Prayer

Say-It Faith—The Objectifying Faith Principle

Knowing God Through Fasting

Rivers of Revival

Understanding the Person of God

ELMER L. TOWNS

REVIVAL IGNITERS

EMPHASIZING THE FIRE OF REVIVAL

DESTINY IMAGE® PUBLISHERS, INC.
P.O. Box 310, Shippensburg, PA 17257-0310
"Promoting Inspired Lives."

This book and all other Destiny Image and Destiny Image Fiction books are available at Christian bookstores and distributors worldwide.

For more information on foreign distributors, call 717-532-3040.

Reach us on the Internet: www.destinyimage.com.

ISBN 13 TP: 978-0-7684-6266-1

ISBN 13 eBook: 978-0-7684-6267-8

For Worldwide Distribution, Printed in the U.S.A.

1 2 3 4 5 6 7 8 / 25 24 23 22

Contents

Revival Igniters in My Life

I was saved in a community-shaking revival in 1950 at Bonna Bella Presbyterian Church. The church had an attendance of 30 to 40 people when two brothers, students at Columbia Bible College, became the summer pastors. Bill and Burt Harding shared the pulpit duties. I attended a prayer meeting in June 1950 with my friend Art Winn.

Only about 17 people attended this small prayer meeting, so we gathered behind the pulpit in a large circle. Burt Harding taught with his back to the pulpit, using a chalkboard as he preached. I had never seen anyone outline a sermon as he taught the Bible. *This is refreshing and innovative,* I thought.

When the message was over, Burt erased the board, and prayer requests were listed on the chalkboard: sick people…unsaved people…missionaries. I had never heard that kind of prayer request. *Does he really expect God to intervene?* I asked myself.

We all knelt down, and Burt expected everyone to pray. I don't remember ever kneeling in public before, and I was a little stiff and embarrassed. When my turn came, I prayed as I always had: "Dear Lord, bless the church, bless our parents, bless the children, bless…bless…bless…" It was a meaningless prayer, especially since I was not talking to God, but making a speech to the 17 people who were there.

The Presbyterians of Bona Bella had just built a new concrete block building. The old building could only seat 30 or 40 people; this one would hold more than 200 people. But the new building was still very much a work in progress. The walls were not painted, and the floor smelled of raw acidic concrete. They had installed aluminum-frame windows, but there were no screens.

When the prayer meeting began, there was sunlight outside, but during our prayer time, darkness fell and mosquitoes invaded the church. If the windows were closed, it was stifling hot. When the windows were opened to let the night air in, mosquitoes swarmed into the room. As we ended prayer, swatting mosquitoes, Burt said, "Let's pray for screens for the windows."

No, I objected silently. *You pray for spiritual things, but no one asks God for screens.* I rebelled at the idea of praying for specific material things like screens. Someone ran to count: There were 27 windows in the new church.

Burt erased the chalkboard and wrote, "27 screens."

"Let's kneel again and ask God for 27 screens," Burt instructed.

I wouldn't pray. I didn't like the idea of making prayer into a shopping list.

But God heard and answered those prayers, and when He did, it transformed my thinking about prayer and about God Himself.

The following Sunday, Burt Harding was making announcements in the Sunday school assembly, and he asked, "Are there any other announcements?"

Bo Burroughs owned the general store in Bona Bella—the only store in Bona Bella—and he stood up to say, "If we're going to have a revival meeting, we've gotta have screens on these windows." He explained that the screens would cost about $4.70 each, and offered to donate four screens. When Bo sat down, Mrs. Alcorn stood to ask him, "Can I buy screens for $4.70?"

"Yes, woman, that's what I meant," the cranky store-owner replied.

"I'll buy four," Mrs. Alcorn told the church.

Quickly, Burt Harding pulled the chalkboard to the front of the auditorium. Everyone saw the phrase "27 screens." He began writing names as people volunteered. When we got close to the goal, I put up my hand and said, "I'll buy two." That's the first time I remember giving money directly to God. Previously I had just dropped a dollar into the col-lection plate without thinking about where it was going. But this time, I was giving to God as He answered the prayers of those who had knelt to ask Him for screens.

Going home that day, I thought, *These people can pray and get answers; they must be real Christians.* At the same time, I also thought the reverse: *I can't get answers to prayer, so I must not be a Christian.*

Later I learned that Bill and Burt Harding were praying for my salvation. They announced to the church that they would pray individually or in small groups from 5:00 to 8:00 every morning for revival. Wow—that long!

Bill and Burt were staying in an apartment over a garage in back of Mrs. Alcorn's home on LaRoach Avenue. Men and women on their way to work would quietly pull their cars into the large sandy backyard, and then make their way up narrow steps to a screened porch that hung out over the doors to the garage. On that porch were an old army cot and a metal glider. Bill and Burt would take turns meeting the people, in half-hour shifts. They provided a dog-eared paper listing names of young people to guide people's prayers. Each morning, they would pray for the salvation of around 60 young people: "Save Elmer Towns...save Art Winn...save Anne Perry...save L.J. McEwen." They prayed for several weeks for young people to be converted in that revival.

Bona Bella was on a rural mail delivery route. On about the fourth night of the revival, the mailman went forward for salvation. Afterward, he stood in front of the pulpit to give testimony: "Everyone here knows me. I'm your mailman, and I know all of you and your box numbers. Each day as I came down LaRoach Avenue toward the church, I felt heat coming from this building. When I passed the building, I felt the heat go away. After two or three days of feeling this heat, I decided to come to the revival and see what was going on."

The mailman continued, "I was raised a Baptist and was baptized by immersion as a young boy. I've been a Baptist Sunday school teacher and deacon, but tonight I was born again. I met the Lord, and He's in my life."

The audience erupted in shouts of "AMEN" and "HALLELUJAH!"

What the postman described as "heat," I would later in life describe as "atmospheric revival." What is revival? It is God pouring His presence out on His people. God's Shekinah glory cloud coming upon the people of the Old Testament was revival. The Holy Spirit coming upon the new church at Pentecost—"I will pour out my Spirit on all flesh" (Acts 2:17, *ESV*)—was revival. The "heat" that the postman felt was the presence of God, which is available to those who are open to Him. God was in that Presbyterian church changing lives, and within a week my life would be changed.

I was converted at a revival meeting at a country church about seven miles away from my home—Bona Bella Presbyterian Church. The little church was experiencing a true Holy Spirit revival.

The revival began during the last week of July 1950; four or five people walked forward for salvation every night. The most startling conversions were Mr. and Mrs. Ernest Miller. (Of their six children, Alyce, the oldest, was already saved. The remaining five were soon to follow their parents.) He was Jewish, and she had been Catholic. About the second night of the revival, she stood up in the small congregation to testify, "I now know the real Jehovah is Jesus who came into my heart." Then she pointed to her Jewish husband, who was too bashful to speak publicly.

"You know my husband, Ernest, is Jewish. Last night he believed in Jesus Christ as the true Jewish Messiah."

The roof was lifted with shouts of *"AMEN!"* A ripple of excitement went through the neighborhood and surrounding Presbyterian churches in Greater Savannah. The revival grew in size and enthusiasm for a week and a half. But then a crisis happened.

No one came forward to be saved on Thursday, July 25, during the second week of meetings. Bill Harding, a junior at Columbia Bible College, a summer pastor of the church, stepped down from the pulpit and stood next to the communion table to announce, "Someone here is breaking the revival." I had been deeply convicted of my sin and felt the urge to go forward—each evening—but had always refused. Bill said, "You're hanging on to the back of that pew so hard, your knuckles are white."

I looked down to see my knuckles clenched around the pew, and instantly jerked my hands away.

"Here's what I want you to do," Bill explained. "Go kneel by your bed, look into heaven and pray, 'Lord, I've never done it before. Come into my heart and save me.'"

That sounded easy, so I determined to do exactly as he instructed. *Maybe this time it will work.*

After church I went out to eat with some friends, so I did not go to bed until around 11:15 P.M. I crashed into bed. When I thought about my sinful condition, I remembered what Bill Harding had instructed. I knelt, looked out the window into heaven, and began talking to God as sincerely as I could—but I couldn't pray what Bill Harding had instructed. I argued with myself: *I've prayed it before—many times—but it didn't work.* So I decided to pray something different—the Lord's Prayer:

> *Our Father, which art in heaven, Hallowed be thy name. Thy kingdom come, Thy will be done in earth, as it is in heaven. Give us this day our daily bread* (Matt. 6:9–11, KJV).

Then I prayed as sincerely as I could, "Forgive us our debts, as we forgive our debtors" (v. 12).

I crawled into bed, still convicted of my sin. I tossed and turned, but couldn't go to sleep. I didn't realize it, but that hot July night, God and satan were wrestling for my soul. Was it possible satan could win? When I couldn't shake off the conviction, I again knelt by my bed, looked into heaven, and was about to pray, "Lord, I have never done it before."

Again I stopped. *It doesn't work, and neither does the Lord's Prayer work.*

Then I remembered what my mother had taught me, so I prayed:

Now I lay me down to sleep, I pray the Lord my soul to keep.

If I should die before I wake, I pray the Lord my soul to take.

I prayed that last phrase several times...very sincerely. I wanted God to take my soul to heaven. Then I climbed again into bed.

The Holy Spirit wouldn't give up. I was more miserable than ever before. So a third time I got on my knees, looked out the window into heaven, and approached God as sincerely as possible. I put all those other times out of my mind and prayed, "Lord, I've never done it before..."

Instantly, the horrors of hell gripped me, as though I were already in flames. Quickly I begged, "Jesus, come into my heart and save me."

That was it. That's all I prayed—and a miracle happened. I immediately knew I was saved. I jumped to my feet and fist-pumped in the dark room, shouting inwardly, *AMEN and HALLELUJAH!*

How do I know I was saved? How does a blind man know when he can see? How does a man know he is wet when thrown into a river? Later I would say, "I know, that I know, that I know." That means first, I knew in my heart (thinking);

second, I knew by experience; and third, I knew innately—just as you know that up is up, and fire is hot.

As I stood in that dark room, I began to sing, "Amazing grace, how sweet the sound, that saved a wretch like me. I once was lost, but now am found, was blind but now I see."

That last phrase explained what happened that evening. I had been spiritually blind, but instantly I had spiritual insight.

Let the Fire Begin

This book is about igniters who started the fires of revival. Remember the word *revival* comes from the word *life*. Revival is living again, or having the former life restored so the person is revived. Revival is God igniting again the original fire on your life that came at your conversion. Revival is re-living the presence of the Lord, so He returns with His excitement of life.

When did the fire first fall—or when did life first come? There are two answers to those questions. Historically, the fire originally fell at Pentecost on the 120 men praying in the Upper Room. Tongues of fire fell on them and they began spreading the fire—spreading the message of Jesus—and the fire eventually spread across to the Roman Empire. Eventually, it spread around the world, touching the United States of America.

But fire can fall a second time. It can re-ignite any group of God's people who have been saved for a period of time. But maybe they have lost the fire and excitement of their original conversion. They still belong to the Lord, but they have lost their "first love" (Revelation 2:4).

There are many ways to start a fire. Look at a pile of dry dead wood. A fire can be ignited carefully with matches or a lighter. Sometimes you see a pile of wood that used to have fire, but now the wood is cold. Fire can blaze up when everyone thought the embers were completely extinguished, or out. Then a new fire can blaze sometimes staring a forest fire.

There are times when a furnace is started with a pilot light. When the thermostat gets chilly, electricity ignites a spark and a fire automatically blazes in the furnace.

Most people don't pay attention to who started a fire, their concern is usually with the fire—how big, how long will it keep me warm, how much will it consume. Most people who study how a fire began want to find out what started the fire, how can we prevent a forest fire from happening again. But now we study the igniters of fire—revival igniters—to find out how to ignite another revival.

What is an igniter? Webster Dictionary defines it, "one who starts a fire, or that which ignites a flame." Therefore revival igniters are those who kindle the fires of revival, or they contribute to the conditions that result in revival fire. Igniters are related to a "cause and effect" action. Those who are igniters either intentionally cause a revival, or what they do spiritually results in a fire, i.e., a revival.

Let's go deeper to ask, "What does it mean to ignite?" Again Webster explains an igniter is a cause of fire, or kindles a fire, or lights a fire that burns. The original meaning of the word igniter goes back centuries, i.e., *to glow* or *to shine*, or the origination of heat. Ah! An igniter will illuminate or is the source of light.

Doesn't the meaning of igniter connect us to our Christian faith? An igniter is one who connects us with God by shining the light of God—or interpreting the meaning of Scriptures.

How do igniters happen? When God's light is shined on a human condition, His light is a contrast with surrounding darkness. The initial entrance of light into a human life makes them uncomfortable with darkness. They see light is good, light helps them, lifts them, and their life is better. Or a biblical term, they are *regenerated*.

Therefore as you read the story of these ten revival igniters, examine carefully how they found the light, what light did to them, how they shined light on others, and how light from the igniters influenced their larger Christian community, then how they influenced the larger Christian world, and ultimately how the light from each igniter influenced history.

Evan Roberts was praying throughout each night until God's powerful transformation reached him, then others. Reports claim over 10,000 were converted because of the

Welsh Revival ignited by Roberts. The revival was spread by two primary sources. First, Evan Roberts and a team traveled among the churches with a message of revival that led to an explosion of all-night prayer meetings. Second, newspapers spread the message widely. The *Western Mail* newspaper said, "He seemed to hold the nation in the palm of his hand."

James McGready, a Presbyterian minister in the American western frontier in Kentucky, was the primary preacher at the Cain Ridge Revival (Second Great Awakening) in the early 1800s. One described his sermons, "My mind was changed by...heaven, earth and hell with feelings indescribable." It began at an annual communion service held with Presbyterian and Methodist churches involved. As McGready concluded, a woman began shouting and singing. Some preachers went to sit beside her, soon the whole congregation was weeping and praying. A Methodist preacher shouted, "Let the Lord God omnipotent reign in your hearts..." McGready went back to comfort the lady, and suddenly, the floor was covered with the slain (people slain in the Spirit). There were people who fell unconsciously to the floor, called, "falling in ecstasy."

News of the meeting spread on America's frontiers. People began arriving on horses and in wagons, coming prepared to camp out as long as revival tarried. It was a few years before these were called "camp meetings." Some estimate 20,000 attended this first camp meeting in Western Kentucky. Within years the meeting attracted 30,000. Then camp meetings spread to the entire Kentucky frontier, followed by spreading to other parts of the United States.

Jeremiah Lanphier was a 49-year-old lay pastor hired by an old Dutch church in New York to do visitation among members. The 88-year-old church was declining, so the leadership thought a door-to-door ministry would revive the church. Lanphier planned a midday prayer meeting for businessmen. He printed and distributed flyers, announcing the first prayer meeting on September 23, 1857, at noon. He waited in vain in the third floor room, looking at his pocket watch, because no one came for thirty minutes. Then he heard footsteps, and six showed up for prayer that day. Prayer was effective. Next week 20 showed up.

Then 21 days later, October 13, the U.S. stock market crashed, banks closed, businesses failed, multitudes were out of work, and the country descended into the worst financial crises ever. New Yorkers flocked to the prayer meetings. The meeting place was changed from one church to another that was even larger. Prayer meetings began springing up all over New York. They spread across America, reaching from Florida to Portland, Oregon. The desperate financial conditions of the depression drove Americans to their knees.

There had been reports of speaking in tongues and Charismatic experiences in a few places before 1906. Some estimate that one half of one percent of American churches were Pentecostal. But when William Seymour, an African-American with no formal education and blind in one eye, began preaching at Azusa Street, Los Angeles in 1906, it began attracting people who came to Azusa Street from all over the world. Then they returned to begin a worldwide movement that approximately 110 years later has influenced about a third of evangelical Christians in the United States. That experience has spread to other nations.

Seymour had heard about a "second work of grace" and asked a friend to pray with him to receive that experience. It came on April 12, 1906. The excited church grew and the news of *glossolalia*, i.e., speaking in tongues, was written up in *The Los Angeles Times*. Although a mostly negative story emphasizing the emotionalism of the Azusa Street, yet the news article caused many readers to come and check out the story. The story of the first glossolalia also appeared in the same issue as the San Francisco earthquake on April 18, 1906. Crowds came to observe or examine or participate in glossolalia. The movement exploded around the city, then the state, and soon around the world.

In 1909 at the Presbyterians' annual meeting of the churches in Pyongyang, Korea, one minister challenged the audience to repent of their hatred for the Japanese who had controlled Korea for a long time. Some signs of revival awakening appeared. Man after man stood to confess their sinful attitude toward the Japanese, and other personal sins. One man threw himself on the ground and beat the floor with an agony of conviction. Then loud screams of agony rang out as one after another broke down in tears to confess sins.

Then the whole audience seemed to break out in audible prayers, everyone praying at the same time. Some loud, others quietly, but many, all praying at the same time. It was both wonderful and indescribable. The meeting went to 2:00 pm. The next evening meeting lasted all night. Some criticized this revival as being "emotional," but it did not include glossolalia. Out of that revival came an explosion of Christianity across Korea. Today Christian church membership represents about a third of the population of South Korea. However, this revival was a middle class movement, while the majority of the lower class remain Buddhist.

The Duncan Campbell revival in New Hebrides, Scotland, 1949, began on the isle of Lewis through the prayers of two elderly sisters in their eighties. They had heard God's Spirit was on a Scottish preacher named Duncan Campbell, so they asked their local pastor to invite him to come to their church for revival. Then they interceded earnestly for an outpouring of the Holy Spirit. When Campbell arrived and preached, revival spread across Scotland, then England and around the world. The prayers of two elderly sisters, Peggy and Christine Smith, ignited the revival. But God used Duncan Campbell as the ignitor of revival.

Billy Graham's name is tied to evangelism more than to revival. J. Edwin Orr was the revival igniter who privately and continually prayed for revival through the Graham crusades. Originally, as a young man, J. Edwin Orr had attempted to walk around the world on faith. He began in his home country of Ireland, crossed Europe, crossed Russia then across China, Japan, Australia. Billy Graham invited Orr to travel to London for the hugely successful 1952 crusade. Orr spent the days and nights of the crusade in prayer.

Orr became a professor of Revivals and Awakenings at Fuller Theological Seminary. As Orr traveled the world studying revivals, he accumulated five doctorate degrees in South Africa, London, Oxford, Chicago, and Los Angeles. Each of his doctoral dissertations examined a different revival in the world. People may forget about his academic achievements and his books on revival, but some credit the private intercession of Orr in hotel rooms with the powerful presence of the Holy Spirit at Graham's early crusades.

Chuck Smith became the revival igniter among the hippie movement that produced the Jesus People also called Jesus Freaks in late 1965. At the time, Chuck Smith pastored a Pentecostal church, i.e., Calvary Chapel in Southern California.

Chuck saw thousands of college students on the beaches of California not far from his home. The mid-1960s saw a flood of bearded kids in ragged jeans, flip flops, shaggy hair. His wife, Kay, challenged him, "Why don't you go down there and be Jesus to them." He at first replied, "They don't need religion, they need a bath!"

That night when Chuck knelt to pray, his prayers could not get through. All he heard was his wife saying, "Be Jesus to them." The next morning again he tried to pray, and again all he heard was, "Be Jesus to them!" That afternoon he put on his swimming trunks, a pullover shirt, sneakers, and went down to the beach with his Bible.

He approached a dozen kids sitting in a circle. They listened intently to his message from the Bible and wanted to do something about Jesus. One of the kids remembered a Bible phrase from his past church days, "Here is water, what does hinder me from being baptized." When Chuck Smith baptized the first one, hundreds gathered—watching, listening, believed, were saved and baptized.

That afternoon revival ignited a group of hippies. It began spreading primarily among the youth, and out of it grew Bible studies—saved hippies gathered in rented properties, boys separated from girls. Chuck Smith's Pentecostal church became a megachurch. They left traditional church music of hymns accompanied by organs and pianos for guitars, drums, and new innovative praise/worship music. Chuck Smith's Calvary Chapel has spread across America to over 2,000 churches. The revival spirit of born-again hippie music has influenced almost all evangelical church music.

Twin brothers—preachers—ignited revival into a Christian and Missionary Alliance Church in the prairies of Western Canada in the mid-1970s. Beginning in an average sized church auditorium, revival moved to the biggest sanctuary in town, and finally filled nightly the massive city auditorium.

Jerry Falwell ignited a revival in a new independent Baptist church plant in Lynchburg, Virginia, with powerful gospel preaching that resulted in people getting saved, so the church was filled more than once on Sunday. Falwell's motto, *Saturation Evangelism*, "Using every available means, to reach every available person, at every available time," actually was more than a description of soul winning; it described his open heart to use as many outreach methods as possible to reach as many unsaved people as possible. Liberty University grew out of aggressive evangelism and ongoing revival to eventually enroll over 100,000 students both in residence and online. The influence of the university produces over 15,000 graduates a year—many going into ministry to spread the influence of super aggressive churches around the world.

Making Fire

Experts describe three necessary elements to start or kindle a fire, i.e., oxygen, fuel, and ignition (fire or spark). All three are necessary, and without these three you won't have fire. These three make a tringle that is called a *fire-triangle*. A fire cannot be ignited or started, or combustion does not happen without all three.

First, fuel is absolutely necessary, and usually it is wood or an oil product, such as gasoline. But also it includes dried vegetation or any combustible product. As long as there is available wood to be burned, a fire can continue to burn. Without fuel you cannot start a fire, and without the availability of more fuel, a fire will extinguish itself.

Air or oxygen is the second indispensable element of fire—air gives life to a fire. Fire cannot burn in a vacuum, it takes air to start a fire or keep it going.

The third element is ignition. When a spark or intense heat is added to fuel where oxygen is available, a combustion or oxidization occurs which ignites the fuel.

Just as there is a *fire-triangle*, so there are three elements necessary for *revival-triangle*. Just as wood, spark, and air (oxygen) is necessary to produce fire, three elements are necessary for revival. First, people ignite the fuel of revival. There must be a movement among God's people (dedication or surrender). God's people are the wood or fuel of revival. Next, fire must have air or oxygen (the Holy Spirit) to give life to revival. The more the Holy Spirit is present the greater the revival. The third element is spark, which represents the presence of God. Throughout Scriptures when God shows up there is fire. It is seen in various manifestations, i.e., shouting, crying, preaching, physical shakers, falling out, and/or intense physical or emotional response.

A fire must have fuel. Sometimes fuel is described as wood, timber, dry vegetation, gasoline, oil products, etc. These represent people who are dry spiritually, perhaps a dead church environment, or a group of people, sinful, evil, and not at all committed to God, yet they are empty, dry, and ready for new life or revival.

The second element for fire is air or oxygen. This is the Holy Spirit moving in revival, prayer, fasting, seeking, repentance and/or waiting on God, which are necessary forces to move the Holy Spirit to pour out revival on a person or group of people.

Sometimes one person may ignite fire, but passes the flame to another who spreads the fire, resulting in a forest fire, or area wide revival. Such was the case of J. Edwin Orr who traveled with Billy Graham in his early evangelical meetings. While Graham preached to thousands, Orr was praying in his hotel room, or was in his private cabin on board an ocean liner. Was J. Edwin Orr the igniter of the revival spread by Billy Graham?

Daniel Nash pastored a small church in upstate New York and was identified as the prayer intercessor behind the massive revival ministry of Charles Finney in America's Second Great Awakening. The people of his church were so irritated by Nash's frequent trips to go intercede behind the scenes for Finney's revivals that they voted him out of his church with a 9 to 3 majority. Nash arrived several days before Finney's revivals, found a small room or space to pray. Then he prayed and fasted for revival, spending most of the day in prayer. Then Nash prayed for others to join him in intercession for revival. He would beg/summon the Holy Spirit to transform the church where Finney was preaching, then he prayed for the community, then he asked God to pour out revival.

Another group of revival igniters were called *watchers* who met together in the church basements beneath the auditoriums where Charles Spurgeon was preaching.

These watchers interceded for revival around the world through the worldwide ministry of Charles Spurgeon.

Chapter 1

Evan Roberts:
The Welsh Revival, 1904

Influencing the World

The Revival in Wales in 1904 influenced the world. It spread from Wales to Scotland and England, and from there, around the world. As the message of revival spread, historian J. Edwin Orr describes the revival as "the farthest reaching of the movements of general awakening, for it affected the whole of the evangelical cause in India, Korea and China, renewed revival in Japan and South Africa, and sent a wave of awakenings over Africa, Latin America and the South Seas." Visiting pastors from Norway, Japan, America, India, South Africa, and Korea attended the meetings and were all deeply moved by the Welsh Revival and became "carriers of revival" to their nations. While the revival influence of Azusa Street was Pentecostal, the influence of the Welsh revival was Evangelical.

The Revival's Impact

With regard to the impact of the revival on the wider culture, historian J. Edwin Orr has noted the influence in Wales:

> Drunkenness was immediately cut in half, and
> many taverns went bankrupt. Crime was so
> diminished that judges were presented with
> white gloves signifying that there were no cases
> of murder, assault, rape or robbery or the like
> to consider. The police became unemployed
> in many districts. Stoppages occurred in coal
> mines, not due to unpleasantness between
> management and workers, but because so
> many foul-mouthed miners became converted
> and stopped using foul language that the horses
> which hauled the coal trucks in the mines could
> no longer understand what was being said to
> them (J. Edwin Orr, *The Flaming Tongue: Evan-
> gelical Awakenings*, 1900 [Chicago: Moody, 1975],
> 192-193).

Evan Roberts attended a Seth Joshua meeting in New
Quay Church, Ireland. At a pre-breakfast meeting on
Thursday, September 29, 1904, the evangelist concluded,
crying out in Welsh, "Lord, bend us." When Evan Roberts
later recalled that morning, he explained, "It was the Spirit
that put the emphasis on 'bend us.'"

"That is what you need," said the Spirit to Evan Roberts. He began praying, "O Lord, bend me."

The motto of the revival in Wales was born out of Roberts' experience: "Bend the church and save the world." Though still young, Evan Roberts was about to become God's agent to carry the spirit of revival throughout his homeland.

Although twenty-six years old, Roberts had just begun his course of study to train as a minister. As a boy growing up in Loughor, Wales, he'd had a compelling desire to "honor God in every aspect of his life." He knew God was calling him into the ministry, but he resisted enrolling in a formal course of instruction, fearing the training might quench his zeal for souls. He testified:

> One Friday night last spring, when praying by my bedside before retiring, I was taken up to a great expanse—without time and space. It was communion with God. Before this I had a far-off God. I was frightened that night. So great was my shivering that I rocked the bed, and my brother, took hold of me thinking I was ill. After that experience I was awakened every night a little after one o'clock. I was taken up into the divine fellowship for about four hours. What it was I cannot tell you, except that it was divine. About five o'clock I was again allowed to sleep on till about nine. At this time I was again taken up into the same experience as in the earlier hours of the morning until about twelve or one o'clock.

At the end of October, Roberts took the train home to be with his family and conduct a week of meetings among the youth in his home church. When he arrived in Loughor, he went to his pastor to request permission to conduct the meetings. The first meeting was scheduled Monday night after the regular service. He was given permission to speak to any youth who agreed to stay after the usual Monday evening meeting.

At the meeting, Roberts urged that "any who were unwilling to submit to the Holy Spirit" should be free to leave the meeting. As a result, only seventeen remained to hear him. For almost three hours, the zealous evangelist led the group in worship and prayer, calling on God to break down any hardness of heart that might hinder revival. During the meeting, the convicting power of the Holy Spirit gripped the audience. They confessed their sins, called on God for mercy.

The results that evening convinced Roberts revival would come in its fullness to Loughor. Attendance began to increase each night. By Friday, those attending included people from several other congregations in town.

He decided to continue the meetings a second week. Furthermore, he would expand the ministry beyond Loughor to other nearby chapels. Without any formal publicity, by Wednesday people were crowding the church, and those who arrived late stood in the vestibule to listen through the open doors.

On Thursday evening, a service was held in Brynteg Chapel in Gorseinon. Many went directly to the church from work to insure they would get a seat. A newspaper reporter wandered into the service two hours after it began. In his story, published in the *Western Mail* on Saturday, November 12, he reported:

> The proceedings commenced at seven o'clock and they lasted without a break until 4:30...on Friday morning. During the whole of this time the congregation were under the influence of deep religious fervor and exaltation. There were about 400 people present in the chapel when I took my seat at about nine o'clock.... There is nothing theatrical about [Roberts'] preaching. He does not seek to terrify his hearers, and eternal torment finds no place in his theology. Rather does he reason with the people and show them by persuasion a more excellent way. I had not been many minutes in the building before I felt that this was no ordinary gathering. A spontaneous impulse of the moment. The preacher walked up and down the aisles, open Bible in hand, exhorting one, encouraging another, and kneeling with a third to implore blessing from the throne of grace.
>
> Seven and a half hours after the meeting began, a woman praying...fainted...the only thing she wanted was God's forgiveness. A well-known resident then rose...salvation had come to him. Immediately a thanksgiving hymn was sung, while an English prayer from a new convert broke

in upon the singing. The whole congregation then fell upon their knees, prayers ascending from every part of the edifice, while Mr. Roberts gave way to tears.

When the reporter left about 4:30 the next morning, dozens of people still stood outside, "discussing what had become the chief subject of their fives."

Two days later, Roberts was invited to preach at Bryn Seion Chapel in Trecynon, Aberdare. He immediately accepted and asked several friends from Loughor to assist him in the campaign. Once again, the Holy Spirit was poured out and the church experienced a significant reviving. By the time the campaign ended, powerful revivals were being reported throughout the nation.

Chapter 2

James McGready:
The Cane Ridge Revival, Western Kentucky, 1800

Beginning the Second Great Awakening

The Cane Ridge Revival began what historians called the Second Great Awakening in the United States.

When the Cane Ridge (Kentucky) Revival began in 1800, conviction was often accompanied by weeping, shouting, fainting, or the "jerks." Crowds met in fields and forests because there were no churches big enough to accommodate them. The "camp meeting," a familiar American revival tradition, was born at Cane Ridge.

The awakening in Virginia, the Carolinas, and Georgia crossed racial and denominational lines. As many as ten or fifteen thousand would gather in forest clearings at camp meetings for the preaching of the Scriptures. Both black slaves and white slave owners from every church background came together to be moved by the Spirit of God.

The Cane Ridge Revival actually began in a communion service at the Red River Church near the Tennessee-Kentucky border. Reverend James McGready was preaching a Friday-to-Monday meeting. Nothing unusual happened on Monday. Then a woman at the far end of the house gave vent to her feelings in loud cries and shouts. When dismissed, the congregation showed no disposition to leave, but many of them remained, silently weeping, in every part of the house. The ensuing revival was described this way:

The methods and spirit of that meeting were repeated in other meetings. Pastor Barton W. Stone soon "learned how to do it" and organized the Cane Ridge services. The zeal of that meeting has never been forgotten:

> It was his [the Methodist preacher's] duty to disregard the usual orderly habits of the denomination, and [the preacher] passed along the aisle shouting and exhorting vehemently. The clamor and confusion were increased tenfold: the flame was blown to its height: screams for mercy were mingled with shouts of ecstasy, and a universal agitation pervaded the whole multitude, who were bowed before it as a field of grain waves before the wind.

Such "agitation" was to become a hallmark of the Cane Ridge Revival.

God on the Frontier

At the end of the Revolutionary War, only 40,000 settlers were located in the hills of western North Carolina, Tennessee, Kentucky, and the area called the Appalachian Region. But within fifty years, more than a million people moved west, seeking free lands, a new life, and freedom. These people needed structure and civilization, but most of all they needed God.

The Methodist circuit preachers organized themselves into societies and brought God to the frontier. Eventually, the camp meeting became popular. It offered a break from hard, backbreaking work, monotonous days, and lonely separation from civilization. One observer described a typical camp meeting this way:

> The glare of the blazing camp-fires falling on a dense assemblage of heads simultaneously bowed in adoration and reflected back from long ranges of tents upon every side; hundreds of candles and lamps suspended among the trees, together with numerous torches flashing to and fro, throwing an uncertain light upon the tremulous foliage, and giving an appearance of dim and indefinite extent to the depth of the forest; the solemn chanting of hymns swelling and falling on the night wind; the impassioned exhortations; the earnest prayers; the sobs, shrieks, or shouts, bursting from persons under intense

agitation of mind; the sudden spasms which seized upon scores, and unexpectedly dashed them to the ground—all conspired to invest the scene with terrific interest, and to work up the feelings to the highest pitch of excitement.... Add to this, the lateness of the hour to which the exercises were protracted, sometimes till two in the morning, or longer; the eagerness of curiosity stimulated for so long a time previous; the reverent enthusiasm which ascribed the strange contortions witnessed, to the mysterious agency of God; the fervent and sanguine temperament of some of the preachers; and lastly, the boiling zeal of the Methodists, who could not refrain from shouting aloud during the sermon, and shaking hands all round afterwards.

According to a pastor at the scene, "the number of persons who fell" was "the astounding number of about three thousand."

The preaching at the Cane Ridge camp meeting and other places was intense, hot, and moving. An eyewitness remembered:

As the meetings progressed and the excitement grew more intense, and the crowd rushed from preacher to preacher, singing, shouting, laughing, calling upon men to repent, men and women fell upon the ground unable to help themselves, and in such numbers that it was impossible for the multitude to move about, especially at night, when the excitement was the greatest, without trampling them, and so those who fell were gathered up and carried to the meeting house, where the "spiritually slain," as they called them, were laid upon the floor. Some of them lay quiet, unable to move or speak; some could talk, but were unable to move; some would shriek as though in greatest agony, and bound about "like a live fish out of water."

No doubt the more "respectable" folks who heard such an account were scandalized, but those who took part were convinced that God was at work.

"Shouting"

The Cane Ridge Revival introduced the element of shouting to revival meetings, so that many were called "shouting Methodists." So many of their new songs had the word "shout" in the words that it became a common religious expression. When someone died, for example, the Methodists said, "He went off shouting."

Shouting was not simply noise, nor was it loud preaching; yet when a minister was preaching, some would shout from the audience. Shouting wasn't exhorting, nor praying, nor was it a united cheer of many believers. Shouting was an individual response. Loud praying was "shouting," as when a congregation all prayed loudly at the same time, when, for example, they attempted to "pray down" a sinner, so he would get converted.

Shouting was praising or rejoicing in God. It was accompanied with clapping of the hands. Shouting became a revivalistic phenomenon; added to it was shuffling of the feet, which was then followed by running around and an occasional leap. Some shouters would "run the aisle." A circular march by the congregation was called a "ring shout."

Other Revival Activities

The Cane Ridge Revival popularized other revival activities as well:

> Singing was attended with a great blessing. At every meeting, before the minister began to preach, the congregation was melodiously entertained with numbers delightful singing.
>
> Shaking hands while singing furthered the work. The ministers...go through the congregation and shake hands with the people while singing. And several...declared that this was the first means of their conviction.

Giving the people an invitation to come up to be prayed for...the ministers usually would tell the congregation that if there were any persons who felt themselves lost and condemned, under the guilt and burden of their sins, that [they could] come near the stage and kneel down...[people] would come and fall down at the feet of the ministers and sometimes twenty or thirty at a time.

Above a hundred persons...came forward, uttering, howling and groans, and on the word, "Let us pray," they all fell on their knees. But this posture was soon changed...they were soon lying on the ground in an indescribable confusion of heads and legs...they soon began to clap their hands violently.

Those who were subjected to the "jerks" acknowledged that it was "laid upon them" as a chastisement for disobedience...the quickest method of warding off the jerks was to "voluntary dance."

Shouting and heartfelt singing, hand shaking and clapping, altar calls and dancing, "jerks" and "falling in the Spirit"—all these extraordinary responses to God's presence soon seemed ordinary in the Cane Ridge Revival.

Chapter 3

Jeremiah Lanphier:
The Fulton Street Prayer Meeting, 1857

Great Revival Before the Horrible Civil War

B y the 1850s, the United States had come to a spiritual, political, and economic low point. Agitation over the slavery issue bred political unrest, and civil war seemed imminent. Then, in 1857, a financial panic, banks failed, railroads were bankrupted, factories closed, and unemployment increased. Many Christians realized the need for prayer in such dire situations.

How It All Began

In 1857 Jeremiah Lanphier, a Dutch Reformed home missionary, began a lay prayer meeting in the Fulton Street

Church of New York City, which began with only six in attendance. Within a few short months, however, the little prayer meeting sparked an awakening that eventually spread across America and around the world. This revival period takes its name from that meeting. There was no leading preacher through whom God brought revival, nor were there great crusades. Instead, this was a movement of lay people who simply prayed, and in response, God worked in their lives and communities in remarkable ways.

In New York City in 1857, the Fulton Street Church (Dutch Reformed) hired Jeremiah Lanphier as a missionary to those working in the city who were unreached by the church. Not quite sure how to proceed in his new ministry, Lanphier decided to organize a noon hour prayer meeting for businessmen in the neighborhood. He printed an invitation to take part of the lunch hour to gather for prayer in a designated room at the Fulton Street Church. Then he distributed the flyers on the street to as many as would take them. On the appointed day, he set up the room and waited.

Twenty minutes after the prayer meeting was scheduled to begin, no one had arrived. Then a few steps were heard coming up the stairs. By the end of the hour, only six had attended the first noon hour prayer meeting at Fulton Street.

In the weeks following, the numbers attending began to increase. By October, the weekly meeting had turned into a daily prayer meeting attended by many businessmen.

By year's end, the crowd had grown to fill three separate rooms in the church.

Similar prayer meetings were organized throughout New York and in other cities across America. By March 1858, front-page stories in the press claimed that 6,000 people were attending noon hour prayer meetings in New York, and another 6,000 in Pittsburgh. In the nation's capital, prayer meetings were conducted five times during the day to accommodate the crowd. As the movement spread from city to city, it became increasingly more common to see a sign posted in various businesses throughout the city: "Will open at the close of the prayer meeting."

Throughout February 1858, Gordon Bennett of the *New York Herald* gave extensive coverage to the prayer meeting revival. Not to be outdone, the *New York Tribune* devoted an entire issue in April 1858 to news of the revival. The news quickly traveled westward by telegraph. This was the first awakening in which the media played an important role in spreading the movement.

In all the major cities of the Eastern seaboard, the lay prayer meetings flourished. Taking up the challenge of Christ, who once asked the apostle Peter, "Could you not watch with Me one hour?" (see Matthew 26:40), most of the prayer meetings were held for exactly one hour, from noon until 1:00 P.M. Many factories began to blow the lunch whistle at 11:55 A.M., allowing workers time to dash quickly to the nearest church (since the revival crossed denominations, they didn't have to attend their own churches) so they could pray for one hour. The whistle then blew again, signaling them to resume work, at 1:05 P.M.

The prayer meetings were organized in the cities by laypeople and were interdenominational. With earlier awakenings, preaching had been the main instrument of revival, but this time prayer was the tool instead. The meetings themselves were very informal—any person might pray, exhort, lead a song, or give a word of testimony, with a five-minute limit placed on each speaker. In spite of the less structured nature of the prayer meetings, they lacked the extreme emotionalism that some had criticized in earlier revivals.

By May 1859, 50,000 people had been converted to Christ through the prayer revival that began at Fulton Street. Newspapers reported throughout New England that there were no unconverted adults in any towns. In addition to an unknown number of nominal church members won to Christ by the revival, more than a million unchurched Americans were converted to Christ and added to church membership rolls. The movement seemed to be God's call to America to repent before the Civil War, in which more Americans were killed than in any other of the nation's wars.

Chapter 4

William Seymour: The Azusa Street Revival, 1906

Spread Pentecostalism Around the World

One of the first igniters of revival is William Joseph Seymour, who many believe was the founder/orig-inator of the contemporary Pentecostal church revival circling the world today. While there were Pentecostal churches in existence before Seymour, the movement was hardly a blip on the attendance scale of American Christianity. But Seymour—an African-American—took courageous steps to pursue the gift of tongues. While he did speak in tongues, he was not the first in the United States to do so. But after the manifestation of tongues at the Apostolic Faith Mission on Azusa Street in Los Angeles, there was an explosion of the larger Pentecostal church movement around the world.

A front page news article in the *Los Angeles Times*, April 18, 1906, gave credibility to the fact Seymour had begun speaking in tongues only a few weeks earlier. In less than 125 years the growth of Pentecostalism is testimony to both Seymour's unique contribution and the evidence of New Testament revival.

Today approximately 25 percent of Protestant Evangelical Christianity around the world is identified with Pentecostalism. At least 19 of the major Pentecostal denominations trace their roots to Azusa Street and the Apostolic Faith Mission.

William Joseph Seymour had come to Los Angeles to preach, but found the church doors were locked. He'd traveled from Texas to Southern California at the invitation of the pastor, but the message he preached had caused the pastor to change her mind. The views espoused by Seymour were questionable at best, at least in the pastor's mind. There was no way she would allow that message to be preached in her church. She couldn't stop Seymour from preaching, but she could and would stop it from being preached in her church.

Still in his mid-thirties, Seymour was well acquainted with rejection. He had begun life as the son of recently freed slaves in Centreville, Louisiana. The South was in transition following the Civil War, but despite the liberation of slaves, in 1870 when he was born, it was a society still steeped in class distinctions.

In those days, receiving a good education was nearly out of the question for an African-American. If Seymour was going to learn how to read and write, he would have to teach himself. The fact that he did so is a commentary on his strength of will and determination.

In his twenties, Seymour left the South and headed north to Indianapolis. For several years, he waited on tables in a prominent hotel. By the time he was thirty, he was living in Cincinnati.

Early in life, Seymour had been drawn into the Holiness movement then sweeping through the South. In Indianapolis he attended the local Methodist Episcopal church, a church that emphasized the ministry of Christ indwelling the life of the believer. He'd been "saved and sanctified" through the ministry of a revivalistic group called "the Evening Light Saints."

This latter group believed human history was coming to an end and anticipated Christ's imminent return to establish His kingdom. Just before that happened, the group believed, there would be a fresh outpouring of the Holy Spirit, a "latter rain" (see Hosea 6:3). To prepare for this, the group encouraged Christians to leave existing denominations to become part of a pure and interracial church God was beginning to raise up.

Speaking in Tongues

Despite the attractive interracial idealism of the Evening Light Saints, Seymour soon found himself back in Houston in a black church. He had little choice; if you were black and attended church, you attended a black church. It was while in this church that Seymour witnessed something he'd never before seen—he heard a woman praying in what seemed like another language.

It was widely held by Holiness groups of that day that "speaking in tongues" was a sign that would accompany the arrival of the last days.

Seymour sensed this woman had something he longed for but hadn't yet found. He knew he had to talk with her.

When he met Lucy Farrow, the woman who had spoken in tongues, he learned she had recently worked as a governess in Topeka, Kansas. Her employer had been a man named Charles Fox Parham, a white preacher who ran a Holiness Bible school, Bethel College, in the same city. Parham had introduced her to the experience he called "the baptism of the Holy Ghost," which led to speaking in tongues.

Before long, Seymour headed to Topeka. When he found Parham, he begged to be admitted into the school.

While Parham was always looking for students and welcomed the zeal of Seymour, Parham was also a Ku Klux Klan sympathizer. He wasn't sure he was ready to welcome a black student into his school. On the other hand, how could he turn him away? That just didn't seem to be the Christian thing to do, either.

Parham allowed Seymour to listen to his lectures from a chair outside by an open window. In the event of rain,

Seymour would be allowed to move his chair into the hall, and the door would be left ajar so he could hear.

Seymour agreed to the terms and earnestly sought the "baptism of the Holy Ghost," but without success.

On to California

A lady visiting from Los Angeles heard Seymour preach and recommended him to her pastor back home in California. Seymour was invited to preach in a little storefront church in California that had been started as a split from a local black Baptist church over the doctrine of the second blessing. When the invitation arrived, Seymour saw it as his own version of the apostle Paul's "Macedonian vision" calling him to a new place of ministry. He borrowed train fare from Parham and made his way west.

At his first meeting, Sister Julia W. Hutchins, pastor of the church, recognized significant differences between the preaching of Seymour and her own views of the second blessing. She considered Seymour extreme in his doctrine of the Holy Spirit, perhaps even heretical. It was clear the two could not continue to work together.

When Seymour arrived at the church to preach at an afternoon meeting, he found the church doors locked. He was no longer welcome in the little storefront church on Santa Fe Avenue. Undaunted, he agreed to preach in a home on Bonnie Brae Avenue.

Several from Sister Hutchins' church attended the meeting along with others in the shabby neighborhood north of Temple Street. Most of the congregation was composed of domestic servants and women who took in laundry. As word of the home meetings spread, the crowds grew. People came to hear a preacher who had never spoken in tongues tell how the blessing of God would come soon when all would have this unique gift.

As Seymour was preparing to go to the meeting on April 9, 1906, an acquaintance named Edward Lee told him he'd received a vision. He claimed the apostles had come to him and told him how to receive the gift of tongues. Together the men prayed, but nothing happened. That night, "the power fell" on those assembled and several, including William Joseph Seymour himself, began praising God in "unknown tongues."

The Apostolic Faith Mission

As news of the outpouring spread through the community, the little home on Bonnie Brae Avenue soon became too small. The weight of the crowd gathered on the front porch was so great, the porch collapsed.

An abandoned church building at 312 Azusa Street was available. It had most recently been used as a warehouse and livery stable. The building was swept out, and

Seymour's Apostolic Faith Mission moved to its new home on Easter Saturday, April 14, 1906.

Seymour preached an apocalyptic message, assuring his listeners the end of the world was at hand. It was his view that Jesus was coming very soon to judge the world and establish His kingdom on earth. Prior to that coming, there would be a "latter rain" outpouring of the Holy Spirit. The evidence that the Spirit had indeed come would be "speaking in tongues."

Then, on the morning of April 18, 1906, four days after the Apostolic Faith Mission had begun holding services on Azusa Street, nine days after the first manifestation of tongues in their midst, the earth itself shook. A major earthquake along the San Andreas Fault almost completely destroyed the city of San Francisco. Its impact was felt throughout Southern California. As the ground shook beneath their feet, the lives of many who had ignored Seymour's message were shaken also.

Daily services at 312 Azusa Street quickly filled with both blacks and whites seeking salvation and "the baptism of the Holy Ghost." One white preacher from the South commented, "The color line was washed away by the blood" of Christ. As the young church witnessed what they perceived to be evidences of the end of the world, their worship of God was noisy and enthusiastic.

A skeptical reporter with the *Los Angeles Times* heard about the meeting and attended. The next day, his report described "wild scenes" and a "weird babble of tongues."

He was the first of many to publish negative descriptions of the revival. But not all who investigated the story left as antagonistic. Before long, reports were being circulated in Pentecostal circles of those who "came to scorn and stayed to pray."

News of the Azusa Street Revival soon began drawing others from across America and around the world. Seymour himself began publishing an occasional paper describing the progress in the spread of his Pentecostal message. *The Apostolic Faith* attracted readers across America and beyond. In it, Seymour described the doctrines of the movement and published reports of tongue-speaking around the world.

As many as 300 soon crowded into the forty-by-sixty-foot frame building. On occasion that crowd doubled, forcing worshipers to gather in the doorway and around the building outside. Many who came to investigate the revival were themselves touched and received the Azusa Street blessing. They became the pioneers of the Pentecostal movement of the twentieth century.

In their earliest days, the meetings at Azusa Street were multiracial in character. Though Seymour initially taught that speaking in tongues was the evidence of the baptism of the Holy Spirit, he felt increasingly uncomfortable with Christians who spoke in tongues yet still harbored racial prejudice toward people of color. He soon began preaching that the dissolution of racial barriers "was the surest sign of the Spirit's Pentecostal presence and the approaching New Jerusalem." Unfortunately, not everyone in the

emerging Pentecostal movement agreed. His emphasis on "race" diluted his message on the Holy Spirit, a few
churches splintered off and the size of the crowds at Azusa
Street went down.

Emerging Pentecostal Denominations

Several major Pentecostal denominations, including the
Assemblies of God in Springfield, Missouri, trace their his-
toric roots to the impact of the Azusa Street Revival on their
founders. Leaders of a black denomination who called
themselves simply "the Church of God" attended the Azusa
Street church for several weeks in June 1907; they returned
home to transform their entire denomination into what is
still the largest black Pentecostal denomination in America, the Church of God in Christ.

Another Church of God denomination, this one white,
became Pentecostal when G.B. Cashwell, an Azusa Street
convert, described the Azusa Street Revival at the national
convention of that denomination. During that meeting,
the General Overseer of the group of churches, A.J. Tomlinson, listened attentively. Then, suddenly, Tomlinson fell
out of his chair and began speaking in tongues at Cashwell's feet. By the end of the century, the Church of God
of Prophecy was a fast growing white denomination in
America.

The influence of the Azusa Street Revival spread far beyond the national boundaries of America. The Pentecostal Assemblies of Canada recognize their spiritual indebtedness to Seymour and the Azusa Street mission, especially in the earliest manifestations of charismatic phenomena in Winnipeg and Toronto. Many of their founding fathers first experienced the Pentecostal blessing under Seymour's preaching, or were mentored by him in their early Pentecostal experience.

The spread of the Pentecostal message to South Africa also grew out of the Azusa Street Revival. John G. Lake visited the Azusa Street Mission prior to taking the Pentecostal message to South Africa in 1908. Within five years he'd established 500 black and 125 white Pentecostal churches in that nation. Others took the Pentecostal message to Europe and Asia.

> The movement crossed the water on both sides to the Hawaiian Islands on the west, and England, Norway, Sweden, and India on the east.... We rejoice to hear that Pentecost has fallen in Calcutta, India.... We have letters from China, Germany, Switzerland, Norway, Sweden, England, Ireland, Australia, and other countries from hungry souls that want their Pentecost.... In Stockholm, Sweden...the first soul came through tonight, receiving the baptism with the Holy Ghost with Bible evidence.... In Christiana, Norway—God is wonderfully demonstrating His power.

Seymour himself died in 1922. The Azusa Street church was closed a few years later, demolished to make way for a new plaza, but the influence of the Azusa Street Revival has been felt around the world now for over a century.

Chapter 5

Presbyterian Missionaries: The Korean Pentecost, 1907

Changing a Nation Forever

Although Korea was one of the last nations in the Far East to hear the gospel, a series of revivals early in the twentieth century quickly turned the Korean church into one of the most powerful forces for God in the Orient. These awakenings transformed Korean culture and society and reached beyond its borders to other nations in Asia.

Visiting South Korea

My first exposure to the Korean Revival of 1907 was in 1978 when I visited South Korea for the first time. I focused my study on the revival of the church *after* the Korean War (1950-53), it was then I learned of the 1907 Revival.[1]

In 1890, Dr. R.A. Hardie, a Canadian Colleges medical missionary, arrived in Korea, a nation that was just beginning to hear the gospel from foreign missionaries. In 1898, he associated with the Methodists. About that time, missionaries first began reporting a turning to Christianity on the part of Korean nationals. While missionaries rejoiced in the interest shown, they lamented the fact that these new converts showed no evidence of conviction of sin followed by repentance and saving faith. It appears the first "converts" were entering the church "as interested disciples rather than regenerated members."[2]

In August 1903, seven missionaries gathered in the city of Wonsan for a week of study and prayer. Dr. Hardie confessed he "had not seen any examples of plain, unmistakable, and lasting conversion"[3] in his thirteen years of ministry in Korea. Believing the ministry was being hindered by his own failings, he confessed his faults before both the missionaries and the Korean congregation, with others making similar confessions.

Just a few months later, in October of 1903, missionary advocate Fredrik Franson arrived in Korea and was invited to preach. The meetings were marked by open confession of sins. Many admitted to theft and offered to make restitution. Church members insisted that restitution be made to the Lord rather than to themselves. As a result, funds were raised for evangelism in the area. During his stay in Korea,

Franson impressed upon Hardie and his fellow workers the necessity of prevailing prayer.

In 1905, Japan's victory over Russia resulted in the Japanese occupation of Korea, provoking a new Korean nationalistic spirit. Christians looked to the church to organize resistance. Instead, missionary and church leaders preached forgiveness and forbearance. This preaching was followed by a second wave of revival in 1905 and 1906, described as "a spreading fire" and "a continuing religious awakening."[4]

Hundreds were converted, more than in any previous year in the history of the Korean mission. In Pyongyang, 700 conversions were recorded in a two-week period. Still, the best was yet to come.

The blessing of God continued in 1906. In Pyongyang, a New Year's Day evangelistic crusade drew 4,000 people to the meetings, 20 percent of the city's entire population. A united evangelistic thrust in the nation's capital, Seoul, resulted in 1,000 conversions.[5]

As had been their custom in recent years, the missionaries gathered at Pyongyang for a week of prayer and Bible study in August 1906. Speaker Dr. Howard Agnew Johnston told Korean missionaries of the Welsh Revival and other awakenings in India.[6] Half of the missionaries then in the nation were Presbyterians and were deeply moved by accounts of revival among Welsh Presbyterians and Presbyterian missionaries in Asia.

News of the other revivals motivated missionaries to intensify their prayer for a similar outpouring in Korea. Throughout the fall of 1907 and the following winter, missionaries gathered in the church each morning at five o'clock to pour out their hearts to God. During one week together, the missionaries studied the First Epistle of John, which later became their textbook for revival.[7]

The New Year's Day Bible Conference

It was the custom of the Korean church leaders to gather at Pyongyang each New Year's Day for a ten-day Bible conference. In January 1907, 1,500 men gathered together, representing the leadership of hundreds of churches. For almost six months, missionaries had been praying for a mighty movement of God among the Korean church, and anticipation grew as the meetings began.

On Monday afternoon, several missionaries gathered together for prayer. They pleaded with God to move among them. One of their number later testified, "We were bound in spirit and refused to let God go till He blessed us."[8] That night as they entered the church, it seemed the entire building was filled with the presence of God.

After a brief message, Mr. Lee, a Korean leader, took charge of the meeting and called for prayer. So many men wanted to pray that Lee announced, "If you want to pray like that, all pray." Across the church, the whole congregation began praying at the same time.[9]

The result was not the confusion one might expect, but rather, as one observer noted, "a vast harmony of sound and spirit, like the noise of the surf in an ocean of prayer." (Later this practice came to be called a "concert of prayer.")[10] In the midst of the prayer, many of the men became deeply convicted of their sin. One after another rose to his feet in deep agony to confess his sins and cry out to God for His mercy.

On Tuesday, the missionaries gathered at noon to discuss what had happened the night before. Only a few had been present at the meeting. One who had been present expressed a personal concern, because it was common knowledge that two church leaders had a hostile relationship.

On Monday evening, a Mr. Kang had confessed his hatred for a Mr. Kim, but Kim had remained silent. Several missionaries were concerned about Kim's unwillingness to reconcile. That evening, God answered the prayers of the missionaries in a most unusual way.

As the meeting progressed, Kim sat with the elders behind the pulpit with his head bowed. Suddenly he came to the pulpit. Holding it firmly, he confessed, "I have been guilty of fighting against God. I have been guilty of hating not only Kang You-moon, but Pang Mok-sa." Kim's animosity toward Kang was well known, but Pang Mok-sa was the Korean name of the missionary who had urged others to pray for him.

The revelation of hatred toward the missionary came as a complete surprise to all gathered. Turning to the missionary, Kim continued. "Can you forgive me?" he asked. "Can you pray for me?"

The missionary stood to pray in Korean. He began, "Apage, Apage" ("Father, Father"). That was as far as he got. "It seemed as if the roof was lifted from the building and the Spirit of God came down from heaven in a mighty avalanche of power among us," the missionary later reported. "I fell at Kim's side and wept and prayed as I had never prayed before."[11]

Across the auditorium, hundreds stood with arms stretched out toward heaven calling on God. Others lay prostrate on the floor. Hundreds cried out to God for mercy.

While they had been praying for revival for months, when it came the missionaries were terrified. Many in the church were in deep mental anguish. Others struggling to resist God were seen clenching their fists and banging their heads against the ground.

Some feared that allowing the meeting to continue would result in some people going crazy, yet they knew they dared not interfere with the work of the Holy Spirit. Finally, they agreed to end the meeting at two o'clock in the morning, six hours after it had begun. Throughout the rest of the conference, similar events were repeated daily.

The Impact of the Revival

The deep reviving of the Korean church leadership had an immediate impact on both the churches and the communities those churches sought to reach. The men returned to their homes as *carriers of revival*.[12] When the story of the Bible conference revival was retold, a similar revival swept the churches.

As the churches were revived, they were gripped by a burning passion to reach the lost in their community. Everywhere, revived churches began to see "drunkards, gamblers, adulterers, murderers, thieves, self-righteous, Confucianists and others" transformed into new creatures in Christ.[13]

The revival had an almost immediate impact in the nation's Christian colleges. Ninety percent of the students at Union Christian College in Pyongyang professed conversion in February 1907. Many also sensed God's call upon their lives as evangelists. They carried the revival beyond the city and into village churches throughout Korea.

From 1905 to 1910, the Korean churches recorded 79,221 additions in membership. That was more than the total number of Japanese church members after fifty years of missionary effort. It was also twice the number of Chinese Protestants after eighty years of missionary labors. By 1912, there were about 300,000 Korean Protestant church members in a nation of twelve million people.[14]

The Korean Pentecost was quickly recognized as a movement of God by Christian leaders around the world. The Edinburgh World Missionary Conference of 1910 declared, "The Korean Revival...has been a genuine Pentecost, for Korean church membership quadrupled in a decade."[15]

The Student Volunteer Movement, an American voluntary association promoting world missions, cited six evidences of "the present day work of the Holy Spirit in Korea" the same year. These evidences included: "(1) the unity and cooperation which prevailed among Christians, (2) the remarkable numerical growth of the churches, (3) the wonderful religious awakening of 1907 which affected 50,000 converts, (4) the noteworthy interest in the Word of God, (5) the dedication of national Christians to service, including generous giving, and (6) the wonderful prayer life of the Korean Church."[16]

Prayer and Fasting

The Korean Revival was born out of intense prayer, and prayer remained an integral part of Korean church life throughout the twentieth century. In many churches, "concerts of prayer" are still practiced in Sunday morning services, with the whole church confessing their sins to God and then calling on God in unison for His blessing. In what have come to be called the "Dawn Meetings," many Koreans still gather every morning at their churches at five o'clock for prayer. Friday nights are devoted to all-night prayer meetings.

Fasting with prayer is widely practiced. More than 5,000 "prayer mountains" have been established—mountain retreats where Christians go for days or weeks of prayer. The prayer life of the Korean church remains a role model for Christians around the world. No wonder that by the year 2000, a third of the Korean population had become members of a Christian church.

Endnotes

1. My first book on revival was *The Ten Largest Sunday Schools* (Elmer Towns, Grand Rapids, MI, Baker Book House, 1969), which focused on the Baby Boomer Revival (1965-1975) which included a study of the growth/revival of Yonggi Cho and the Full Gospel Church, Yoido Island, Seoul, South Korea. My next book was *Rivers of Revival* (Neil Anderson and Elmer Towns, Ventura, CA, Regal Books, 1997). Anderson focused on revival within the individual and I focused revival in the church and culture. My third book was *The Ten Greatest Revivals* (Elmer Towns and Douglas Porter, Richmond, VA, Academx, 2005).

2. Elmer Towns and Douglas Porter, *The Ten Greatest Revivals Ever* (Virginia Beach, VA: Academx Publishing Service, Inc.), 41.

3. Ibid.

4. Ibid., 16. Revival is described as "An evangelical revival is an extraordinary work of God in which Christians repent of their sins as they become intensely aware of his presence in their midst, and they manifest a positive response to God in renewed obedience to the known will of God, resulting in both a deepening of their individual and corporate experience with God, and an increased concern to win others to Christ."

5. Ibid., 42.

6. Ibid.

7. Ibid.

8. Ibid., 43.

9. Ibid.

10. Ibid., 44.

11. Ibid.

12. Ibid., 44. A *carrier of revival* is a term introduced by J. Edwin Orr that means a person takes a torch of fire from a revival and begins another similar experience in another place by testimony or sharing reports of the original revival. Because there are several types of revival, a *carrier of revival* reproduced the same elements of revival. There are at least nine different "faces" of revivals listed in *Rivers of Revival* (Neil Anderson and Elmer Towns, Ventura, CA, Regal Books, 1997, 116-117): Blessing encounter, Deeper life encounter, Truth encounter, Sin encounter, Worship encounter, Holy Spirit encounter, Conversion encounter, Culture encounter, and Power encounter.

13. Ibid., 18. Was the Korean Revival a major revival? The book *The Ten Greatest Revivals* lists questions to ask when determining the greatness of a revival. (1) Does the experience fit the biblical portrait of revival? (2) Was there a

demonstration of God's presence? (3) Was the larger body of Christ awakened to its New Testament tasks? (4) Was the surrounding culture impacted positively by the revival? (5) Are there reliable sources that demonstrate the greatness of the rival?

14. Ibid., 45.

15. Ibid.

16. Ibid.

Chapter 6

Duncan Campbell: New Hebrides Revival, 1949

Revival Spread to Neighboring Nations

C hurch attendance was in decline after World War II. Not a church in the Hebrides Islands off the coast of Scotland could boast of having a single young person attending Sunday services. Instead, the youth of Scotland flocked to "the dance, the picture-show and the drinking-houses."

Peggy Smith, an eighty-four-year-old blind prayer warrior, and her sister Christine, ailing with severe arthritis that left her in pain most of the time, were the human instruments responsible for revival. The two sisters were no longer able to attend services, but their humble cottage just outside of town had become a sanctuary of prayer for revival. As the two sisters prayed together, blind Peggy had a vision of the churches crowded with youth, and sent for her minister.

The Reverend James Murray MacKay visited the two shut-ins and listened intently to the account of the vision. His own wife had had a similar dream only a few weeks earlier. Neither the pastor nor his wife had told anyone of the dream, but Peggy's vision confirmed it. The pastor knew what he had to do next.

Reverend MacKay called his leaders to prayer. For three months, they prayed two nights each week among bales of straw in a local barn. They asked God to send revival.

After several months, a young deacon rose in the meeting one evening and began reading from the Scripture: "Who may ascend into the hill of the Lord? Or who may stand in His holy place? He who has clean hands and a pure heart" (Psalm 24:3-4). He paused, closed his Bible, and began to speak.

"It seems to me so much humbug," he said, "to be waiting and to be praying, when we ourselves are not rightly related to God." Then, lifting his hands toward heaven, he prayed, "O God, are my hands clean? Is my heart pure?"

The words had barely come out of his mouth when he went to his knees and fell into a trance. Some observers mark that night as the beginning of the New Hebrides Awakening.

Even so, Pastor MacKay knew he needed help. He considered inviting Duncan Campbell, an experienced Scottish revivalist, to preach in his parish. Then MacKay received word that Peggy Smith wanted to see him again.

God had told her in prayer to have Pastor MacKay invite Duncan Campbell to preach. "God is sending revival to our parish," she insisted, "and he has chosen Mr. Campbell as his instrument."

So, the two agreed, and MacKay invited Campbell for ten days of meetings. This evangelist had been raised in the Highlands of Scotland and spoke fluent Gaelic, had a burden for the Gaelic-speaking people of the Highlands and the islands. Yet, even though he was willing to minister in Lewis, he had other commitments. Campbell thus declined the invitation but agreed to come a year later if the invitation were still open.

MacKay wasn't sure what to think when he received Campbell's response. He believed that God was about to send revival to the area, and wanted Campbell to be a part of it. The difficult task that now faced him was communicating the bad news to Peggy.

"That's what man says," Peggy replied, "God has said otherwise! Write him again! He will be here within a fortnight!"

Unaware of these events in the town of Lewis, Campbell was beginning to wonder whether he'd done the right thing in turning down the invitation to preach. He felt strongly impressed by God to accept the invitation he'd rejected, but the decision had already been made.

About the time Peggy Smith and her sister began praying for revival, God began preparing Duncan Campbell for the revival. At home he was preparing a sermon in his study when a granddaughter asked him, "Why doesn't God do the things today that you talk about in your sermons?"

The child's question brought deep conviction on Campbell. He shut the study door and fell on his face before God, praying, "Lord, if you'll do it again, I'll go anywhere to have revival."

A little time later he sat in the front row getting ready to preach at the famed Keswick Bible Conference. It was the opportunity of a lifetime; a place Campbell had always dreamed of preaching.

Nevertheless, the Holy Spirit told him to leave immediately and go to the New Hebrides Islands to accept the invitation he had previously turned down. Turning to the moderator, Campbell excused himself, saying, "Something has come up; I must leave immediately." He left the building and did not preach what he thought was the opportunity of a lifetime. He caught the next ferry to New Hebrides.

As Campbell stepped off the ferry, he didn't look well. Crossing from the mainland to the island on a choppy winter sea had left him sick. The church elders did not know he was coming, but God told them to meet the ferry that came only once a day. He was sick and they thought he would be unable to preach that night. Yet preach he did, drawing from the parable of the ten virgins, challenging

Christians concerning their responsibility toward those who were "asleep in sin."

The next night, according to one report, "a solemn hush came over the church as Campbell preached." After the benediction, the people left. As Campbell stepped out of the pulpit to leave as well, a young deacon raised his hand, moving it in a circle. "Mr. Campbell," he began, "God is hovering over us. He is going to break through. I can hear already the rumbling of heaven's chariot-wheels."

At that moment, the door opened and the clerk of the session (the church elders) beckoned to Campbell, calling, "Come and see what's happening!" When he went outside, he discovered that the entire congregation had remained outside the church. Others had joined them as well, drawn from their homes to the church by some irresistible force they couldn't explain. One youth who was at a dance suddenly quit dancing and fell to the floor in a trance. He went to the church and all the others followed. The faces of more than 600 people in the churchyard were marked by deep distress.

Suddenly, a cry from within the church pierced the silence. One young man, agonizing in prayer, had felt such intense anguish that he fell into a trance and lay prostrate on the floor. The crowd streamed back into the church, filling the building beyond its capacity.

A witness later recalled: "The awful presence of God brought a wave of conviction of sin that caused even mature Christians to feel their sinfulness, bringing groans

of distress and prayers of repentance from the unconverted. Strong men were bowed down under the weight of
sin, and cries for mercy were mingled with shouts of joy
from others who had passed into life.

"Oh, praise the Lord!" a woman cried out. "You've come
at last."

Peggy and Christine Smith, though still at home, also
shared in the revival that night. "We had a consciousness of God that created a confidence in our souls which
refused to accept defeat," Peggy explained the next day.
She told how she and her sister "struggled through the
hours of the night, refusing to quit praying." They reasoned:
"Had God promised, and would He not fulfill?" So far as the
Smith sisters were concerned, the New Hebrides Awakening was a "covenant engagement," God's faithful keeping
of a promise.

The revival spread quickly to neighboring districts, "traveling faster than the speed of gossip," according to one
observer. Campbell received a message one night that a
nearby church was crowded at one o'clock in the morning
and wanted him to come. He arrived to find a full church
and crowds of people outside.

Two hours later, Campbell was called to a group of more
than 300 people who were still praying in a nearby field.
Unable to get into the church, they had begun their own
prayer meeting.

In the village of Arnol, people were generally indifferent
and opposed to the revival. Nevertheless, a prayer meeting

was organized there. Shortly before midnight one night, one of the men present stood to pray. As he prayed, the room in which they met shook as "wave after wave of divine power swept through the house, and in a matter of minutes following this heaven-sent visitation, men and women were on their faces in distress of soul."

The New Hebrides Awakening had a significant impact on life throughout the island. In one village, "the power of God swept through the town and there was hardly a house in that village that didn't have someone saved in it that night." On Sundays, the rural roads of these remote islands were crowded with people walking to church. Drinking houses, which were common before the revival, remained closed for a generation following it.

Chapter 7

Billy Graham:
The Los Angeles Crusade, 1949

Beginning of Worldwide Evangelism

B illy Graham, president of Northwestern College, Min- neapolis, Minnesota, had accepted the invitation to preach a Los Angeles evangelistic crusade, but first he was to speak at an annual briefing for Christian col- leges held at Forest Home, a Christian retreat in the San Bernardino Mountains outside Los Angeles. At that con- ference, he spoke several times with Henrietta Mears, the director of Christian education at First Presbyterian Church in Hollywood, California. A dynamic Christian, Mears had led the growth of that church's Sunday school from 175 students to more than 4,500 in only a few years.

Mears sitting at the dinner table talked with Graham about his commitment to revival. At the same table, J.

Edwin Orr, a leading authority on revivals and professor at Fuller Theological Seminary, challenged Graham to consider the possibility that God might spark a national revival through the latter's preaching at Los Angeles.

The third person at the table was Chuck Templeton, an evangelist who had attended Princeton University in the Ph.D. program and accepted the "new" theology of German theologian Karl Barth. Because Templeton had developed a liberal interpretation of Christianity, he questioned Graham on the inspiration and authority of God's Word. Chuck criticized Graham, Orr, and Mears, saying, "Billy, you're fifty years out of date. People no longer accept the Bible as inspired. Your language is out of date. You're going to have to learn new jargon if you're going to be successful in your ministry."

That night, Graham walked under a full moon in the hills of the San Gabriel Mountains where he dropped to his knees, opened his Bible, and prayed, "O Lord, there are many things in this book I do not understand...there are seeming contradictions...I can't answer the philosophical and psychological questions Chuck and others are raising...Father, I'm going to accept this as Thy Word by faith...I will believe this is Thy inspired Word." It was there in that private midnight prayer meeting Billy met God and prayed for revival for the coming Los Angeles crusade.

Graham called this a life-changing event. His faith newly secured in the Word of God, he would ever after "pepper" his sermons with the phrase "the Bible says." With a renewed vision of revival, Graham left the retreat center spiritually ready for Los Angeles.

Graham approached the Los Angeles crusade with an invitation from a group of businessmen representing a loosely organized association of 200 churches called "Christ for Greater Los Angeles." He later wrote in his best-selling book *Just As I Am*: "I burned with a sense of urgency... that if revival could break out in Los Angeles...it would have repercussions around the world."

Because of this conviction, Graham had insisted that the committee meet three requirements before he could accept the invitation. They had to broaden support for the crusade to include all churches and denominations, raise the budget from $7,000 to $25,000, and erect a tent for 5,000, rather than for 2,500 as they had proposed.

Given these terms, many had criticized Graham for being "a self-promoting money-grabber." Yet Graham had maintained faith that God would do a new and greater work than before. At that time, most evangelists would have been considered successful if fifty people were converted and more than 2,000 attended. The committee had finally agreed to his conditions, and the campaign was set to begin in the last week of September and to run for three weeks.

As the crusade began, Henrietta Mears had Graham present a series of Bible studies to Hollywood stars and songwriters in her home off Hollywood Boulevard. J. Edwin Orr moderated these Bible studies, again pressing the need for revival. Also attending was Stuart Hamblin, a West Coast radio legend whose popular radio show was heard up and down the Pacific Coast for two hours every afternoon. Hamblin quipped that he could fill the tent if he endorsed the crusade.

Graham conducted a news conference with the local media before the crusade began, a strategy he'd never taken before. The next day there was nothing in the paper except for a paid announcement about the crusade. Stuart Hamblin interviewed Billy on his radio show and told his audience, "Go down to Billy's tent and hear the preaching," adding, "I'll be there."

That night Hamblin attended, but he angrily stomped out in disagreement with the message, though in reality he was under conviction. This episode was repeated two or three more times. Finally, Hamblin and his wife, Suzie, came to Graham's hotel at 4:30 in the morning, where Hamblin gave his heart to Christ. Later, Hamblin would write the well-known songs "It Is No Secret (What God Can Do)" and "This Ole House."

Graham had been praying about extending the crusade, and the conversion of Stuart Hamblin was his sign from God to continue. When he arrived at the tent that night, reporters were crawling all over the place. William Randolph Hearst, owner of two newspapers in Los Angeles and a string of newspapers across the country, had been quoted as saying, "Puff Graham" (that is, "make this story big").

Some in the media claimed that was the cause for the success of the crusade. In response, Graham said the credit belonged to the work of God in the hearts of the multitudes, not Hearst. While the organizational committee had expected fifty conversions in three weeks, that many were being converted every evening.

The newspapers ran the story because something unusual was happening. Stories ran in Detroit, New York, and Chicago as well. *Time Magazine* reported:

> Bland, trumpet-lunged North Carolinian, William Franklin Graham, Jr., a Southern Baptist minister... dominates his huge audience from the moment he strides on stage to the strains of *Send a Great Revival in My Soul*. His lapel microphone, which gives added volume to his deep cavernous voice, allows him to pace the platform as he talks, rising to his toes to drive home a point, clenching his fist, stabbing his finger at the sky, and straining to get his words to the furthermost corners of the tent.

The headlines announced, "Old-Time Religion Sweeps Los Angeles."

The next sensational conversion was that of Jim Vaus, a wire tapper for the mob, who worked for Mickey Cohen, a high-profile local mob boss. That event not surprisingly hit the headlines. When Graham visited Cohen's home to present the gospel to him, Cohen rejected the appeal, yet even Graham's visit there made headlines.

The Associated Press put out a daily press release on the events of the crusade that was printed in almost every newspaper in America. The meetings went on for seventy-two nights, and thousands were converted, 82 percent of whom had never made a profession of faith.

The Los Angeles crusade kicked off sixty years of crusades by Billy Graham. Millions made professions of faith. Every major city in America held a Billy Graham campaign, and he preached around the world as well. More than one million in a single audience heard him in person in Seoul, South Korea. The conditions were ripe for a work of God after World War II, and Billy Graham was the man God used to bring, as the title of his book described it, *Revival in Our Time*.

Chapter 8

Chuck Smith:
Jesus People Revival,
1965

Igniter of Charismatic Movement

News of the Jesus People Revival broke across the country in the mid–1960s when full-page photographs appeared in *Time*, *Life*, *Newsweek*, and *Look* magazine. One memorable picture showed the glistening, tan body of a long-haired hippie emerging from the waters of the Pacific, smiling because he'd just been baptized after receiving Christ as Savior. Chuck Smith, pastor of a Pentecostal church, was leading a Southern California movement to win the counterculture youth who were flocking to the beaches of Southern California.

One day Chuck Smith, a Pentecostal pastor in Costa Mesa, California, and his wife sat in a coffee shop watching a California beach that was populated with youthful bodies "as far as the eye could see." Chuck commented to his wife, "They need to get saved." His wife answered, "Why don't you go down there and be Jesus to them."

He laughed off the comment. That night when he prayed before going to bed Chuck had in his mind, "Why don't you go down there and be Jesus to them." He put it out of his mind and went to sleep.

The next morning he heard the same words in his mind again. That afternoon Chuck went down to the beach in a swimming suit, shirt, and shoes—with a Bible. He walked up to several youth talking in a circle.

"Can I tell you about Jesus?"

They listened intently and as he was sharing the gospel, some were saved. Then one of them asked, "Here is water, what doth hinder me to be baptized?" Apparently the boy had a church background and understood the question from the New Testament.

Chuck put the Bible down and took of his shoes and wadded into the Pacific Ocean and began baptizing the young people in that circle. Others began running up to ask what was going on. He preached to a growing crowd. That day he baptized over 100 young people who had prayed to receive Christ. The same thing happened day after day.

Chuck Smith's congregation grew, the hippies over-flowed the traditional crowd of about 100 Pentecostal worshipers, which consisted of older folks in suits, ties, and dresses, along with the hippies in shorts and flip flops. They moved from an old church building to a rented Lutheran church, then to an abandoned school, to ten acres, where they pitched a tent that would seat 2,200. Then they built a new auditorium where I attended the Sunday night service in 1977. They ushered me to the second row; some hippies sat on the floor to make room for me.

The church was winning more than 200 to Christ each week. In a normal month, about 900 were baptized in the Pacific Ocean, with crowds of over 3,000 spectators. The highly visible occasion was used to preach the gospel and win more to Christ. Eventually, Smith's congregation grew to fill four separate services each Sunday and became one of the twenty largest churches in the world.

Eventually, the church acquired a Christian communal house where those converted could live and be discipled. No more drugs and free sex—the houses taught them discipline, soul-winning, and ministry. The first hours of every morning were given to Bible study, the afternoons to beach evangelism, and the evenings to rallies and evangelistic Bible studies.

The Jesus People revolution was more than a California phenomenon. Another group recruited from countercultural ranks, calling themselves the Jesus People, left Seattle, Washington, and traveled to Milwaukee, Wisconsin, to begin Jesus People Milwaukee. There were also the Jesus People Chicago, and yet another group, Jesus People USA. Jesus People revivals began spreading throughout Michigan, Illinois, and Wisconsin, and finally to Florida.

What kind of youth became part of the Jesus People revival? Every kind—college students and high school dropouts, church kids and kids with no church background, youth with relatively "straight" backgrounds and youth who had tasted the poisonous elements of the sixties culture—drugs, alcohol, "free" sex, the occult. But they all came to know Christ as Savior, and churches who were willing to reach out to them welcomed them with "coffeehouses" and other ministries that made them feel at home.

When attendance at Chuck Smith's Calvary Chapel reached more than 10,000 per week, those young people he trained were sent out to start other Calvary chapels, first in California, then up and down the Pacific Coast, and finally to New York, Florida, and elsewhere. Today the largest church in the northeastern United States is Calvary Chapel of Philadelphia, with more than 10,000 in attendance, pastored by Joe Focht (who was reached on the beaches of California as a youth and trained by Chuck Smith). Now there are more than 1,200 Calvary Chapels, and most of them are large churches, originally pastored by a "hippie convert." According to these church planters, they never intended to start small churches; each set out instead to do a great work for God.

Chapter 9

McLeod/Sutera Twins:
Saskatoon, Saskatchewan, 1971

Influencing Canada

Located in the heart of the Canadian Bible Belt, Saskatoon, Saskatchewan was among the nation's "most Christian cities," with more churches per capita than any other community in Canada. Yet, despite the strong evangelical influence in the community, something was lacking. Several pastors recognized the problem and began praying for revival. Among those committed to seeing God move in his community was the pastor of the local Baptist General Conference church, Reverend Bill McLeod.

McLeod was a student of revival and had often prayed for revival in his own ministry. When it was announced that Duncan Campbell, leader of the New Hebrides Revival, was preaching at a pastors' conference in a neighboring province, McLeod attended the meeting. His heart was stirred as he listened to the stories of what God had done in Scotland.

"If God could do it in Scotland, why not Canada?" McLeod wondered. His conviction that God would indeed do it in Canada was strengthened when Campbell told him of a vision. The Scotsman claimed he had seen a prairie fire starting in Saskatoon that would spread around the world. Both Campbell and McLeod agreed revival would come to Saskatoon, and that the revival would have a global impact.

The pastors of various Saskatoon churches gathered weekly to pray for revival. Beyond that prayer meeting, they also encouraged their churches to pray for revival.

Although there was no significant immediate response, McLeod himself became even more convinced the revival was imminent. He had a unique dream one night in which he believed God was purifying him to be "a vessel of honor" in God's service. As McLeod continued to pray, he heard about the unusual response taking place in the meetings of a pair of evangelists.

Ralph and Lou Sutera were twins serving the Lord together in an itinerant evangelistic ministry. Initially, the Suteras' ministry had not been much different from that of a host of other traveling American evangelists. Then, without explanation, God had begun to move in an unusual way in the churches in which the Suteras preached.

McLeod contacted the Sutera twins and invited them to conduct a campaign at his church, Ebenezer Baptist in

Saskatoon. The meetings began on Wednesday evening, October 13, 1971. From the beginning, it was obvious this would not be a usual "week of meetings."

God began to speak to longtime members about grudges they held toward other Christians. Two brothers who hadn't spoken to each other in several years responded to the invitation one evening to embrace publicly before the church. Barriers that hindered revival were shattered. By the weekend, a spirit of conviction had gripped the church.

The revival was too big not to share with others. McLeod called his fellow pastors to tell them what God was doing. Members of their church began sharing what God had done in their lives with other Christians they knew in town. Attendance at the meetings grew rapidly.

When the crowd outgrew the little Baptist church, they moved the meetings to an Anglican church that seated 700 people. The next night that building was full. Then they moved the meetings to an Alliance church that seated 900 people. That building filled in two days. Next the meetings were moved to a United church in town that seated 1,500 people. Before the Sutera campaign ended, they were meeting in a civic auditorium that could accommodate 2,000 people.

The meetings were conducted every night for seven and a half weeks, usually continuing until ten or eleven in the evening. Following each meeting, many peo-ple stayed for an additional gathering to get right with God. The after-meetings, as they were called, were often characterized by humble confessions of sin and the reconciling of fractured relationships. It was not uncommon to find people still in the prayer room at four or five in the morning.

As Christians returned to the Lord, many of their unsaved friends and family members noticed the change and embraced Christ as Savior. Revival had come to the Canadian prairie.

Before long the unchurched in town began to realize something unusual was happening in Saskatoon. Taxi drivers began getting calls to pick people up at church late into the night. They also got calls from people under conviction, asking the drivers to take them to church late at night.

About half of those converted in the revival were young people. The large numbers of converted youth changed the atmosphere in local schools and colleges. Student rebellion and cheating were transformed into a spirit of cooperation as campus Bible studies and prayer groups began forming.

Businessmen in town also noticed the change. People began paying overdue bills that were about to be written off. Others who had cheated restaurants or hotels returned to pay their bills in full. Shoplifters began returning stolen goods they could not afford to buy. Criminals turned themselves in to the police, confessing their crimes.

Chapter 10

Jerry Falwell:
Revival at Liberty University and Thomas Road Baptist Church, 1973

Foundation for Largest Evangelical University

Revival began at Liberty University in October 1973. There were 600 students at three-year-old Liberty University. Owning few facilities, the school instead used the Thomas Road Baptist Church; the dormitories were in a rented hotel down town and at the church camp on Treasure Island. Classes were taught in an abandoned public school building. Being spread out across town meant there was no place for the students to fellowship or enjoy an easily accessible commons room. Instead, they just hung out in the auditorium of Thomas Road Baptist Church.

After a regularly scheduled Wednesday night prayer meeting, about 35 students lingered in the auditorium, chatting and studying together. A young man walked up to the pulpit. Through his tears he began, "You all know me. You think I am a Christian..." Then he began to confess his sins of cheating and other problems in his life. "I made a profession of faith in my home church, and I was baptized as a boy, but I'm not saved."

The microphone was off, and the platform lights were darkened, so few people noticed the young boy kneeling and weeping uncontrollably. Quickly, several gathered around to pray with him and for him. Two or three other small groups throughout the room stopped and also prayed.

There was rejoicing on the platform stairs when the young man had prayed through to salvation. Then a second young man climbed up to the pulpit and repeated almost the same story. He confessed his sins, telling how he got baptized as a boy, and again asked for prayer, telling the group, "I'm not saved." Several students gathered around him for prayer. He too was converted.

Next a young woman made almost the same confession and the same request. After a while, when the rejoicing settled down, a reverent spirit filled the auditorium; people knew God was present. He was working in the young people's lives.

Someone went to the piano, unlocked the keyboard, and began to play. The music continued without interruption from approximately 10:00 P.M. Wednesday night until 9:00 A.M. Saturday morning, two and a half days. There were always three or four pianists waiting on the first row to slide onto the piano bench to keep the music going. Someone also played the organ during the 59-hour stretch, too.

Young people spontaneously began lining up to the left of the pulpit; they wanted to request prayer for salvation or give a testimony of what God had done in their lives. Around midnight on Wednesday, phone calls went out to pastor Jerry Falwell and the deacons, "Get down to the church fast, revival has broken out." They got there as quickly as possible because the Lord was in the house.

By 6 A.M. the next morning more than 2,000 people had flooded the auditorium. Many church members did not go to work that day. Mothers got together to babysit for one another, and a few businesses closed down. School at Lynchburg Christian Academy cancelled classes. The Lord's presence was experienced in Lynchburg, Virginia.

The first meal served to the University students would have been breakfast Thursday morning. I don't know, and no one remembers if anyone went to the kitchen to prepare it. Did anyone go to the dining room to eat breakfast? That same question could be asked about lunchtime, dinnertime, and every other meal until the revival was over. No one remembers what was happening in the kitchen or dining room; everybody remembers God was moving in the church auditorium. No one would dare leave because they would miss what God was doing. When students could no longer stay awake, they slept under the pews, or on the floors alongside the walls of the foyer.

Some student called for a delivery of pizza. When it arrived, everyone seemed embarrassed to eat. They were too busy with God's work in the church sanctuary. The pizza sat on top of a waste paper receptacle, and eventually was thrown into the trash, uneaten. People were feasting on the Bread of Life, and God was satisfying empty spiritual appetites.

The emotions of the moment take away one's hunger. Think if you were called to the hospital because your spouse or child was in the emergency room. You would dash there as quickly as possible. Even if it were 12 noon, would you drive thru for a hamburger first? "No!" Eating at this critical time is not important. We lose our appetite in times of fear, excitement, and waiting anticipation. We don't want to eat until it's over.

Liberty University experienced a miraculous revival in its early days where many young people met Jesus Christ, and surrendered to fulltime Christian service. Perhaps, God's mighty outpouring of the Holy Spirit was a prediction of the spiritual future of Liberty University. It would produce many thousands of local churches, some of them growing to 10,000 or 20,000 in attendance. And beyond church plant-ers, many thousands became pastors of existing churches, and multitudes became foreign missionaries. Graduates became powerful businessmen and women, leading great enterprises; and then educators at every level from uni-versity presidents and leaders to kindergarten teachers.

And don't forget the political influencers of Jerry Falwell Sr., some Liberty University graduates becoming representatives to the U.S. Congress, plus State Houses, and then city and county officials. The revival in Lynchburg touched almost every area of life.

Devotions

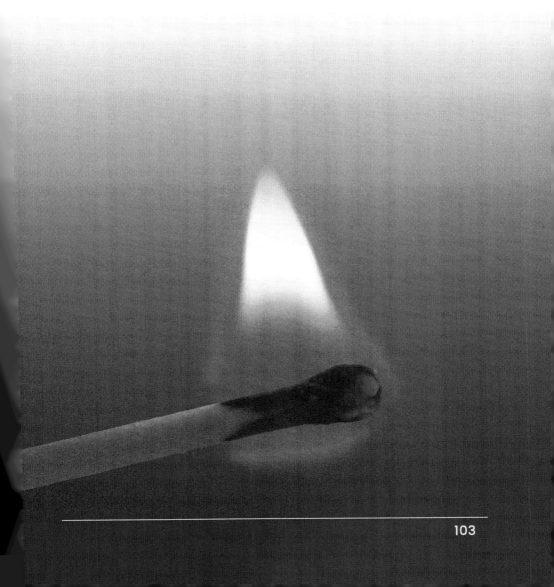

Day 01

The Promise

"I will pour out my Spirit upon all people."
Joel 2:28, NLT

Let's begin with the One making the promise to pour His Spirit on you. God is speaking and He promises to pour out His Spirit—the Holy Spirit—on the needy. Remember in the creation narrative. It was the Holy Spirit who originally gave life to everything, so when you, or any thirsty person, needs revitalizing, God will revive them or you with the undeniable source of life—the Holy Spirit. So, if you need a new start in life, or you just need a "kick-start" for your next challenge, empty your life of anything that hinders the Spirit's free work in your life. Seek His fullness for revival.

Lord, I come to You who saved me from sin and called me to be Your servant. Forgive me of any and all sins. Cleanse me, revive me, and use me. I want to walk with You in full fellowship. Amen.

The word *pour* has two applications. First, look at God who is the Source of pouring the Holy Spirit over us. If you want Him to pour on you, make sure you are in a right relationship with Him. Second, look at the one who received the Spirit—you. If you want reviving from the Holy Spirit, make sure you are in a receivable mode. That means you have done all you have to do to have the Spirit poured on you.

> *Lord, I have confessed my sins and the blood of Jesus Christ has cleansed me (1 John 1:5-10). I believe in the Holy Spirit, and I want Him to be poured out on me. I am ready and waiting. Amen.*

Read: Joel 2:12-32

Outpouring

"Do not leave Jerusalem until the Father sends you the gift he promised."

Acts 1:4, NLT

"They all met together and were constantly united in prayer."

Acts 1:14, NLT

The eleven disciples were in the Upper Room waiting for God to pour the Holy Spirit on them. They were praying. Perhaps a time of individual silent prayer. Perhaps a time of meditation. Perhaps a time of reading a psalm that expressed the prayer of their hearts. Perhaps they all prayed out loud at the same time to God, a latter expression of revivals in Europe and America. But beyond their praying, they were seeking what God promised, i.e., the *outpouring* of the Holy Spirit. Therefore, each were exercising faith that God would do for them what Joel had predicted (Joel 2:12-29) and what Jesus promised.

Lord, pour the Holy Spirit into my life. I need revival and I need a new challenge to serve You fully and to serve You joyfully. Fill me with the Holy Spirit and let Him control my life and flow through me. Amen.

The disciples waited ten days in the Upper Room before the Holy Spirit flooded their lives on the Day of Pentecost. How long are you willing to wait and pray for your personal revival and for revival in your group? Will you do all the things the disciples did as they waited on the Lord? They had the promise of Jesus; why don't you claim that promise? What was written for them can be applied to your life.

Lord, I am waiting for the Holy Spirit to revive me. I want to feel His atmospheric presence. I want His Spirit to revive me with the joy I had when I was first converted. Fill me...fill me new! Amen.

Read: Acts 1:1–2:13

Revive

"During the forty days...he appeared to the apostles from time to time, and he...talked to them about the Kingdom of God. Once when he was eating with them, he commanded them, 'Do not leave Jerusalem until the Father sends you the gift he promised, as I told you before.' ...On the day of Pentecost all the believers were meeting together in one place."

Acts 1:3-4; 2:1 NLT

Would you like for God to revive you personally, or even more, would you like God to revive your group, your church, your community? Notice what the disciples—including a total of 120 people—did to receive the pouring out of the Holy Spirit on the Day of Pentecost. First, they remained where Christ appeared to them. Next, they were united in heart, soul, and prayer. They were all praying for God to fulfill His promise to send the Holy Spirit to be poured out on them. Then they prayed together. Their faith was united in prayer. But it wasn't just one person praying. They all prayed. Isn't that the way to expect revival?

Lord, I come to ask You to pour out the Holy Spirit on me and send revival to me. I will pray for it, wait for it, and seek it. I want a revival to begin— so begin in me. Amen.

When 120 believers were praying for 40 days, that is a lot of people praying a long time. But look at the great manifestation on Pentecost—flaming tongues of fire sat on each, they were filled with the Holy Spirit, they spoke in foreign languages so that many heard the gospel preached by Peter. "And we all hear these people speaking in our own languages about the wonderful things God has done!" (Acts 2:11, NLT). Yes, God did a great work, but the 120 people paid a great price in time, energy, commitment, and faith. Can it happen again? Yes, all things are possible with God.

Lord, I want You to manifest Your Holy Spirit in my life, as great as on the Day of Pentecost. I will pray, sacrifice my time, energy, and life to see it happen. Begin another Pentecost in me. Amen.

Read: Acts 1:12-2:47

Signs from Heaven

"Suddenly, there was a sound from heaven like the roaring of a mighty windstorm, and it filled the house where they were sitting. Then, what looked like flames or tongues of fire appeared and settled on each of them. And everyone present was filled with the Holy Spirit and began speaking in other languages, as the Holy Spirit gave them this ability."

Acts 2:2-4, NLT

God sent three supernatural signs from heaven on the 120 praying at Pentecost. First, it was the sound of a roaring mighty wind that filled the Upper Room. It could be as loud as a tornado, yet there was no physical damage to the room or the house. God was telling them He was sending them power and life and movement. Second, flaming tongues were set on each of them. In Scriptures, fire usually was a sign of purity and cleansing. God was cleaning their tongues, getting them ready to speak for God the message of Jesus' death, burial, and resurrection.

Third, each began to speak in a foreign language. Notice the miracle was in the speech of the 120 witnesses, not in the ears of the listeners. Why? "We all heard these people speaking in our own language about the wonderful things of God" (Acts 2:11, NLT).

> *Lord, thank You for the miracles of Pentecost. I believe what happened then. I pray for revival today. Fill me with the Spirit and use me to witness to others the miracles You have done in my life. Amen.*

One more great event took place at Pentecost. "Everyone present was filled with the Holy Spirit" (Acts 2:4). You don't have to wait for a special prayer meeting. Paul promised you can "be filled with the Spirit" (Ephesians 5:18). Why don't you ask for the Holy Spirit to fill you now?

> *Lord, when I was saved, both You and Jesus came into my heart and life. Also the Holy Spirit came into my life. Now I want the Holy Spirit to take control of my heart and life and use me. Amen.*

Read: Acts 2:1-21

All People

"Those who believed what Peter said were baptized and added to the church that day—about 3,000 in all."

Acts 2:41, NLT

Peter began preaching, "I will pour out My Spirit upon all people" (Acts 2:17). As Peter preached in the language of the Jews of Jerusalem, many heard the message in their own language (Acts 2:11). Various disciples began interpreting—or re-preaching—Peter's sermon in the foreign language given them. The men disciples were re-preaching to groups of both men and women. But there may have been groups of unsaved women that day who heard Peter's re-preached sermon by one of the women leaders that day in the Upper Room (Acts 2:17). They had waited on the Lord and asked to be filled with the Holy Spirit as well. Now, God used believing female followers of Jesus to lead unsaved women to faith in Jesus. Didn't Peter promise the Spirit poured on "all flesh"? Also he promised, "Your sons and daughters will prophesy" (Acts 2:17). Then Peter repeated, "I will pour out my Spirit even on my servants—men and women alike" (Acts 2:18, NLT).

> Lord, thank You for using all to re-preach the sermon on the Day of Pentecost. Thank You for answering their prayers. Now I ask for the Holy Spirit to use me in ministry. Amen.

God was moving evidently in the streets. He was no longer confined to the Holy of Holies in the Temple in Jerusalem. God was using more than Levities who ministered in the Temple. He was using Peter, a fisherman, and other men who worked with their hands. God was using the disciples of Jesus. And God was using women who were re-preaching the sermon of Peter to other women. God was using ordinary people who were followers of Jesus to get over 3,000 additional followers of Jesus.

> Lord, I am ordinary. I yield all I am and have to You. Fill me with the Holy Spirit and use me in Your service as You did at Pentecost. Amen.

Read: Acts 2:1-41

120 Equals 3,000

"Peter's words pierced their hearts."

Acts 2:37, NLT

There were many reasons why this sermon was so effective—over 3,000 were saved and baptized. During the past 10 days the 120 prayed as they waited for the Holy Spirit to come. They also meditated on the truth Jesus gave them, and they thought and studied the Old Testament, especially applying Jesus' promise of the Holy Spirit to Old Testament predictions about His coming. Those Scriptures were on Peter's mind as well as on the minds of those in the Upper Room. Had they discussed it and applied it? Yes, both Peter and all those re-preaching in each foreign language. They had prayed, studied, and were ready with answers for the large group of unsaved Jews.

Lord, thank You for using Peter and all Your 120 followers on the Day of Pentecost. Thank You for their faithfulness. Now, I will faithfully prepare myself so You can use me. I know the opportunity is coming and I will be ready. Amen.

Yes, the 120 followers were ready to share, minister, and preach on the Day of Pentecost. Don't forget about the 10 days of prayer and waiting on God, and asking God to use them as they shared the gospel message given to them by Jesus. They were ready in every way! Mentally, message-wise, faith expectation, and rejoicing in God for the opportunity to minister.

Lord, give me the faith of those who prayed in the Upper Room. I commit myself to the discipline of prayer. Give me success in serving You, and I will faithfully prepare. Give me joy in ministry, for I rely on Your filling for power and results. Amen.

Read: Acts 2:41-47

Make Disciples

"Those who believed what Peter said were baptized and added to the church that day—about 3,000 in all."

Acts 2:41, NLT

"Then the churches throughout all Judea, Galilee, and Samaria had peace and were edified. And walking in the fear of the Lord and in the comfort of the Holy Spirit, they were multiplied."

Acts 9:31, NKJV

It was not enough for unsaved people to become followers of Jesus. He had commanded, "Make disciples" (Matthew 18:19). Once a person became a follower of Jesus, there was an added challenge, "Teach these new disciples to obey all the commands I have given you" (Matthew 28:20, NLT). Multiplication is when each disciple becomes a *disciple-maker* of another new disciple. God built multiplication into the thinking of each disciple. But then, notice the church in Jerusalem became a *church-maker*. Just as a disciple must make other disciples, so a church must produce another church. Challenge your church and yourself, "Are we producing reproducers?"

> *Lord, thank You for my wonderful salvation. I will share it with others. I ask You to help me reproduce my faith in another person, first to help them accept Christ as their Savior, then help me to guide them to share their faith with others. Amen.*

Just as everything that grows from a seed in the ground will produce another plant/fruit like itself, so each believer has the seed of faith that can be planted in another person who can become a Christian just like themselves.

> *Lord, give me the faith to see the potential You have placed within me to reproduce myself in others. May I do it physically, mentally, emotionally, but most of all—spiritually. May I led some new believers to be even stronger in their faith than I am in mine. Amen.*

Read: 2 Timothy 2:1-2; Acts 2:40-47; Acts 9:31

Revive to Live Again

"Will You not revive us again, That Your people may rejoice in You?"

Psalm 85:6, NKJV

"O Lord, I have heard Your speech and was afraid; O Lord, revive Your work in the midst of the years! In the midst of the years make it known; In wrath remember mercy."

Habakkuk 3:2, NKJV

There are several definitions for revival, but today let's focus on a return to the original vigor or strength of spiritual life we originally experienced when we were first saved, or when we first were aware of the new life God had given us at salvation. Do you need a spiritual revival that gives you a new motivation to serve God, something like your new momentum to return to work after a vacation? Is it like getting over a sick spell to get back to the life you enjoyed before illness hit you? Revival is re-igniting your love for Jesus after you have "lost your first love" (Revelation 2:4). Revival is hungering to search the Scriptures to find Jesus in its pages. Revival is a passion to pray and spend time worshiping and praying to the Lord.

Lord, forgive me for any coldness in my heart about spiritual things. I am sorry I don't pray as often or as passionately as I used to do when seeking You. Light a new fire in my soul and re-ignite the fire I had when I was first saved. Amen.

When you feel a need to meditate on Jesus, that is a sign of returning revival. Revival can come after a long time of spiritual laziness—days, weeks, months—or it can come after physical sickness for a brief time. Revival is a renewal of your fellowship with God. Revival could come after your "one day" of wayward actions or wayward thoughts. Revival is renewing your love to the Lord.

Jesus, I come seeking to be drawn close to You as I used to experience Your presence. I want to walk with You in fellowship and talk with You in prayer, and meditate on Your goodness and grace. Draw me close to You and I will come. Amen.

Read: Habakkuk 3:1-18

Revival Refreshing

"Now repent of your sins and turn to God, so that your sins may be wiped away. Then times of refreshment will come from the presence of the Lord."

Acts 3:19–20, NLT

Another definition of revival is "times of refreshing." And what is refreshing? It is when you return to your first love for Jesus when you first were saved. If not that, then it is a return to that event or experience when you fully embraced Jesus. You could feel His presence and you talked with Him and had fellowship with Him. Sometimes when your room or office is musty smelling, you open a window or door to let in fresh air. And what does it do? The room is revival-refreshed. So when you experience revival in your life, what happens? Your life is refreshed with the presence of Jesus. And what is a refreshed room or a refreshed life? It is enjoyable, revegetating, and a new lease on living.

Lord, I come to You because I want "a time of refreshing" in my spiritual life. Help me love You as much as I have in the past. I want to pray in faith as I did in time past. Renew me and renew my walk with You. Amen.

When you ask God to refresh your spiritual life, it is like you putting a new coat of paint on your house. It is like power washing the porch, sidewalk, and driveway. It is like you are looking at your life through new eyes, with new challenges, and you have new energy to meet the new challenge of your life.

Lord, I confess my sinful thoughts and attitudes. Also, cleanse my sinful actions. Refresh my soul and give me new opportunities to live for You and to serve You in new ways. Thank You for the refreshing presence of the Holy Spirit. Ah! It is good to rest in fellowship with You. Amen.

Read: Acts 3:1-25

Times of Refreshing

"That is why the Lord says, 'Turn to me now, while there is time. Give me your hearts. Come with fasting, weeping, and mourning. Don't tear your clothing in your grief, but tear your hearts instead.' Return to the Lord your God, for He is merciful and compassionate, slow to get angry and filled with unfailing love. He is eager to relent and not punish."

Joel 2:12–13, NLT

Do you want spiritual revival in your heart and life? Look at the challenge from Joel. First you must turn to the Lord—now. That means you turn away from any sinful habits or actions. What does God want? "Give Me your heart" (v. 12)? He does not want half your heart, but all of it. He does not want your heart just on Sundays when you go to church, He wants all your heart all the time. How shall you turn? God says with three actions. First, with fasting, meaning you put God before food. You can fast for 1, 3, 10, or 40 days. Let God show you how long. Second, come with weeping. Aren't tears a sign of sincerity? You cry when you are really hurt, or you are really happy. Come to God in that time of full sincerity.

> *Lord, I come to You and turn from everything else. You have my attention. I come to You with tears of rejoicing for salvation and tears of sorrow for not coming sooner. And Lord, I will fast, tell me when and how long. Amen.*

When you "turn to God," you express your sincerity with mourning. You are sorry for your sins and you are sorry for not serving God as best as you could have. You mourn because you could have done more in ministry, or you could have gone deeper in Bible study. But remember, mourning leads to recommitment about those things that make you morn.

> *Lord, forgive me for not studying Your Word more. I recommit myself to more diligent Bible study. Forgive me for not spending more time in prayer and not being more diligent in intercession. I will seek Your presence and I will intercede more deeply. Amen.*

Read: Joel 2:1-32

Pour

"I will pour out my Spirit on all people."
Joel 2:28, NLT

What will God pour on you? His Holy Spirit! When will God pour His Spirit on you? When you meet the conditions of Joel 2, when you begin to experience revival. It starts when your faith reaches out to God because your faith is weak or faltering. Then it continues when you get a vision of what God does for you and all people He receives. Next, your vision turns to desire. You begin to want God's presence, because you have experienced the "husks" of the world, and they do not satisfy your soul. You desire to have the peace of God ruling your heart. But you also want the power of God to give you strength to overcome your weakness and temptations. But most of all you want God's presence—you want God in your life.

Lord, I am empty and needy, I need to be filled with Your presence. I need Your power to overcome temptation. I need Your peace to rule my heart. I need You to fill the empty places in my heart. Amen.

What does pouring represent? You pour from that which is full, and you pour into that which is empty. If you are empty today, God is full. What does God want to do for you? He wants you to testify with Psalm 23:5, "My cup runneth over." Have you ever been completely filled with God's presence—up to the brim? How about overflowing?

Lord, I ask You to pour Your Holy Spirit into my empty heart. I need the Spirit—pour. I want the Spirit—pour. I have faith to receive the Spirit—pour. I will share with others—pour! Amen.

Read: Psalm 23:1-6

The High Holy Place

"For thus says the High and Lofty One who inhabits eternity, whose name is Holy: 'I dwell in the high and holy place, with him who has a contrite and humble spirit, to revive the spirit of the humble, and to revive the heart of the contrite ones.'"

Isaiah 57:15, NKJV

We are a needy people and God is holy and far off. How can we get God in our life? First, you already know to receive Christ as Savior and let Him rule your life from the throne of your heart. But there may be times when you feel He is not near, as Isaiah states that God, "inhabits eternity...dwells in the high and holy place" (Isaiah 57:15). But God can visit you to dwell in your life and make His home in your presence. You need two adjectives, *contrite and a humble spirit.* When you humble yourself, you put God on the throne of your heart (James 4:10). Next you need a contrite heart. Webster said it's "to grieve for a short coming or sin." So, two steps to revival. First, humble yourself and put God on the throne of your heart. Second, grieve over your shortcomings and sins.

> *Lord, I want a revived heart. I want You who "inhabits eternity" to inhabit my heart. I ask forgiveness for my pride and give You first place in all this. Revive me. Amen.*

Contrite comes from the word *grind* as though you have been worn down into the ground. This is a picture of a person who has been stomped into the ground by their sins. The good news of Isaiah is "revive the heart of the contrite spirit" (v. 15).

> *Lord, I need reviving. My sin has worn me down and I am spiritually empty. Fill me with Your Spirit and revive my life. I will rejoice in Your filling. Ah! I love Your Spirit! Amen.*

Read: Isaiah 57:1-21

The Word of God

"The instructions of the Lord are perfect, reviving the soul. The decrees of the Lord are trustworthy, making wise the simple."

Psalm 19:7, NLT

One of the foundational stones of revival is the Word of God. Sometimes the Bible is the beginning of revival when some have read the Bible then sought the Lord and He revived them. At other times the Bible is the end of a person's search for God. They search for the Lord everywhere but find Him in a verse in God's Word. David wrote, "You will be revived when you receive instruction from His Word" (v. 7, ELT). Why is that? Because the Lord's Spirit lives in the Words of Scripture, and the Spirit revives the thirsty or hungry soul. Also, Jesus said, "The words that I speak to you are spirit, and they are life" (John 6:63, NKJV). Remember, the word *revive* means to "live again," so when you get Jesus' Words in your mind and life, you get His life—which is enteral life.

Lord, I am empty and need reviving. I will come to You and read Your Word. I will learn Your Words to learn life. I will meditate on your word, to know life. "I have hidden Your Word in my heart" (Psalm 119:11, NLT) so I have eternal life dwelling in me. Amen.

The Bible is not magic; you won't get spiritual by owning one or just reading it. You must understand the message of the Bible, and apply its meaning to your heart. You must make the living words of God part of your life and everyday living. Then the power of God's life will enter your life. Then the direction of God's Word will guide your life. Then the thoughts of God will influence and control your mind and thinking.

Lord, I need reviving. I will read Your Word to let it revive my spirit. I will meditate on Your Word to let Your ways direct my life. I will let the Bible control my life and decisions, so Your will can influence my life. Then I will be revived and serve You. Amen.

Read: Psalm 19:1-14

Revival Is Restoration

"Will You not revive us again, That Your people may rejoice in You?"

Psalm 85:6, NKJV

Some churches advertise a "revival meeting," but they usually have an "evangelistic meeting" with a purpose of getting people saved. But a true "revival" is when people return to God and put Him first in their life. Sometimes a revival is a return to the original joy and victory over sin when you first got saved. Sometimes revival is a corporate decision to return to when they served Christ as they previously did. Revival is not about church meetings or crusades, revival means when God revives His life in you or the group. It is when God brings you back to your original dedication to Him or the joy of your salvation. Revival has many synonyms—renewed, refreshing, resurgence, rejuvenation—but sometimes it involves restoration when we go back to restore the ways we used to serve God, or we restore the things we promised in the past and did not do. We did not keep our promise to God.

> *Lord, I need revival. Show me any ignorant sins I need to confess. Show me any promises I need to fulfill. Forgive my sins and failures. I want to walk in fellowship with You as I did when I was first saved. Amen.*

Revival is about life—your inner life and daily experiences with God. Revival is not about church meetings; however, God can visit church meetings to revive individual believers. And then, enough of them can revive a church. So, pray for your church to have a revival—where individuals are revived with the presence of God. But, before you pray for others, let it begin with you.

> *Lord, revive me. I want to go back to where I was first saved. Then I want to grow in Jesus. I want Jesus to control my life. Revive me today so I may grow in Christ to serve Him more. Amen.*

Read: Psalm 19:1-14

Your Heart Attitude

"Then Solomon stood before the altar of the Lord in front of the entire community of Israel, and he lifted his hands in prayer."

2 Chronicles 6:12, NLT

Notice Solomon let his physical body reflect the attitude of his heart. He stood at the right place, "before the altar of the Lord." But to get revival fire, he also stood before "the entire community of Israel." Whether all Israel could see him, at least he put himself in a "seeable" place. Why is that? So all Israel could join him in prayer to God, asking for God's presence in the dedication. Next, he "lifted his hands in prayer." Is it important to lift hands or fold hands as you pray? The answer—your outward physical body must reflect the inner person interceding to God. Sometimes you begin with the hands so the physical body will follow in reverence. At other times you begin with inner prayer, and then the outward physical body follows.

Lord, I come praying for revival. I want Your spiritual fire to fall on me. That means spiritual awakening. God, send Your presence as I seek You for revival of my life and service to You. Amen.

But Solomon did not just lift his hands to show his heart was lifted in prayer to God. He knelt. When you kneel before the Lord, you acknowledge His lordship over your life and His control of your prayers and the actions to follow. What you see is a picture of Solomon's complete submission to God. God saw both Solomon's outward and inward submission to Him, then God sent the fire. What will it take for God to send fire/revival into your life?

Lord, I will follow Solomon's example. I lift my hands to You, asking for Your blessing on my life. But I also kneel before You, asking for the fire of revival to revival-kindle my life. Amen.

Read: 2 Chronicles 5:1–6:12

Day 16

Why Revival Fire Fell

"When Solomon finished praying, fire flashed down from heaven and burned up the burnt offerings and sacrifices, and the glorious presence of the Lord filled the Temple. The priests could not enter the Temple of the Lord because the glorious presence of the Lord filled it. When all the people of Israel saw the fire coming down and the glorious presence of the Lord filling the Temple, they fell face down on the ground and worshiped and praised the Lord."

2 Chronicles 7:1-3, NLT

Throughout biblical history, fire has symbolized the presence of God. Why did the fire of God fall? It fell because Israel had done the right thing in praying at the Temple according to specifications. The right man—Solomon—was leading worship. They had the right attitude—prayer! They had built the Temple at the right spot. And the right people were assembled with the right attitude. When everything was right—God's fire fell. If you want revival in your life or you want God to revive your ministry, get everything right. Revival begins with you. You must get right with God (confess sins), seek God's presence (spend time praying), then get others to join you in doing the same preparations that you made.

> *Lord, I will prepare myself for revival. I now confess my sins and ask for cleansing. Give me faith to believe Your promise of power. I will pray for all the ingredients of revival. Revive me! I want Your presence in my life. I seek it and ask You for it... please! Amen.*

Did you see the response of the people when God's fire (presence) fell? They fell on their faces to worship God. You know, worshiping God is associated with revival. If you want the revival fires of God to fall on you, make sure you begin with worship—and you continue worshiping till revival comes.

> *Lord, I bow to Your glory and power. I invite Your revival presence to fill my heart and overflow to those around me. I worship You to receive revival, and I will worship You when revival comes. Amen.*

Read: 2 Chronicles 7:1-22

If

"If my people who are called by my name will humble themselves and pray and seek my face and turn from their wicked ways, I will hear from heaven and will forgive their sins and restore their land."

2 Chronicles 7:14, NLT

Did you see the first word in today's verse? What does "if" mean? It means the conditions for revival must begin with us—His people. God challenges us to do four things. First, we must humble ourselves. That is hard to do because our old "self" is at the center of our personality—life. Second, we must pray. There are many things for which we must pray, but prayer for yourself is primary. Third, seek God's face. That means we put God at the center of our life. When you take "self" out of the center of your life, you allow God to work in your life. Fourth, we must turn from our wicked ways. That means stop doing those things that are sin and start obeying the Lord. If you want revival, these four steps are the place to start.

Lord, I am challenged by the call to revival. I want You to revive my life. Help me as I deal with my pride and self. I will pray for revival and seek Your will in my life. As I repent, help me do a thorough job. Amen.

God promises to do three things when we take steps to revival. He will hear our prayers and forgive our sins. Remember, the depth of God's forgiveness is measured by the depth of our sincerity when we pray and turn to Him. Then God will "heal our land." Which means He will heal our home life, business life, and the rest of our life.

Lord, I need revival and want it deeply. So, I pray sincerely and seek Your revival in my inner life, my family life, my business life—my whole life. Amen.

Read: 2 Chronicles 7:12-22

The Cloud

"At that moment a thick cloud filled the Temple of the Lord. The priests could not continue their service because of the cloud, for the glorious presence of the Lord filled the Temple of God."

2 Chronicles 5:13-14, NLT

God was ready to receive the worship of Solomon, the priest, and the people. So, God showed up in a thick cloud. His presence filled the new magnificent Temple. Why did God show up? Because the people had obeyed and sacrificed to construct the Temple, and because the people came to praise the Lord and magnify Him. If you would do that in your life, God would show up. When revival visits a believer or a group of people, God shows up. Not only were the people and leaders prepared, they had come that day *expecting*. They were *expecting* to please God. When they did all these things God came, but no one could see Him—because God is invisible. He came in a cloud.

Lord, I want revival. I will do all the things You expect so You will be pleased with me and my yieldedness to You. I come surrendering my sins, my ego, my life, my all. Amen.

There is another reason for the cloud. The people expected God to be pleased because they had done their best. It takes faith to please God. "Without faith it is impossible to please Him, for he who comes to God must believe that He is, and that He is a rewarded of those who diligently seek Him" (Hebrews 11:6, NKJV).

Lord, I need faith. I will study Your Word to learn more about You. I will pray more to find Your presence. I am like the man who met Jesus, "I believe, help thou my unbelief" (Mark 9:24). Amen.

Read: 2 Chronicles 5:1-14

Singing

"The priests took their assigned positions, and so did the Levites who were singing, 'His faithful love endures forever!' They accompanied the singing with music from the instruments King David had made for praising the Lord. Across from the Levites, the priests blew the trumpets, while all Israel stood."

2 Chronicles 7:6, NLT

Notice what happened after God appeared in a thick cloud, and then the fire fell from heaven to consume the sacrifices. The people responded with singing! They worshiped singing the psalm, "He is good, His faithful love endures forever" (Psalm 136:1). Then the priests accompanied their singing with instruments, next other priests blew their trumpets. God gives us music for many reasons. One is to worship and praise Him. It is only natural that when God showed up in a thick cloud and fire, the people worshiped Him with music. Do you ever sing by yourself driving the car? Do it to worship Him. If you sing "flat" like I do, don't worry about your musical quality. God responds to a grateful heart who worships in music.

> *Lord, I have been singing since I was a child, but today, I will sing to You. I will sing songs to magnify You and choruses to thank You for saving me. Amen.*

If I had been at the Temple dedication and heard the instruments playing, then joined by trumpets, and finally with the Levitical choir, I would have also sung with them. I love singing to God because my focus is on Him. Isn't that what worship is all about!

> *Lord, I will sing when I have my private devotions early each morning. I will sing as I kneel in prayer at night. Make my life enjoyable like a song. Amen.*

Read: Psalm 136:1-36

Right Place

"Then Solomon stood before the altar of the Lord in the presence of all the assembly of Israel, and spread out his hands."

2 Chronicles 6:12, NKJV

Some think the right place to start a revival is in a church meeting, or in a prayer meeting, or in a needy place where God could make a difference. But the right place for a revival is not found in a building or in geography. The right place for revival is in God's presence. But add to that, you must have the right attitude and the right intercession. Revival begins when your heart is broken for lost people and sin in the church and world. Then revival takes root in fasting and prayer, i.e., agonizing intercession for God to pour His presence on you and your group. Next, add "tarrying prayers" as a key to revival. Time spent in God's presence will begin to unleash rivers of revival.

Lord, I want revival in my group. Start in me, send revival to my soul and life. I will search my heart for hidden sin and repent. I will claim by faith Your promise to "pour out" Your Spirit. I will wait in prayer for Your Spirit. Amen.

When you are "tarrying in prayer," make sure you find God's presence and make sure He is listening to your intercession. Also, ask God to prepare your heart and life for revival. When revival comes, you also get the presence of God. Make sure you are *revival ready* for Him. And when you are ready for revival, remember you are not waiting for a "feeling" or "for religious excitement," you are waiting for God.

Lord, I am waiting in Your presence. Show me anything in my heart that hinders revival. I will confess and claim cleansing by the blood of Jesus (1 John 1:7-10). Lord I am waiting...come. Amen.

<u>Read: 1 John 1:1-10</u>

God Fire

"When all the children of Israel saw how the fire came down, and the glory of the Lord on the temple, they bowed their faces to the ground on the pavement, and worshiped and praised the Lord, saying: 'For He is good, for His mercy endures forever.'"

2 Chronicles 7:3, NKJV

When the fire fell on the altar as Solomon was dedicating the Temple, it was not normal fire—it was God's presence. When Moses and the children of Israel were waiting at the bottom of Mount Sinai (Exodus 19, 20), God manifested Himself on the mountain with fire (Hebrews 12:10-24). Doesn't the Scripture teach, "Our God is a consuming fire" (Hebrews 12:29)? While fire is a symbol of God's judgment, it also is a symbol of cleansing and purity. When you approach God to pray for revival, remember to seek out any hidden sin in your life. Repent and confess it. Get God's cleaning and commit yourself to live a pure-holy life.

Lord, I come praying for revival. Show me any hidden sins. I confess them to You and I repent to live a pure life. I want Your cleansing in my life, I want revival, I want and need Your presence. Amen.

Remember, fire hurts when it burns, so when God's fire falls on your life, it will hurt. Sometimes it hurts emotionally, sometimes it hurts financially, sometimes you have to repent and change things in your life. To be clean and pure within, fire has to burn away all impurities and uncleanness.

Lord, I come asking a hard thing. I ask You to cleanse me within. I will repent without. I want to be a clean empty vessel for You to indwell. I want Your presence in my life. Amen.

Read: Hebrews 12:18-29; 13:10-25

Listener's Outlines

A Revived Church

"Those who believed what Peter said were baptized and added to the church that day—about 3,000 in all. All the believers devoted themselves to the apostles' teaching, and to fellowship, and to sharing in meals (including the Lord's Supper), and to prayer. A deep sense of awe came over them all, and the apostles performed many miraculous signs and wonders. And all the believers met together in one place and shared everything they had ...all the while praising God and enjoying the goodwill of all the people. And each day the Lord added to their fellowship those who were being saved."

Acts 2:41-46, 47, NLT

A. First Church Began with Revival

1. _____ ? "I will pour out my Spirit upon all people" (Joel 2:28, NLT).

2. _____ . "Do not leave Jerusalem until the Father sends you the gift he promised" (Acts 1:4, NLT). "They all met together and were constantly united in prayer" (Acts 1:14, NLT).

3. _____ . "All the believers were meeting together in one place" (Acts 2:1, NLT).

4. _____ : (1) Wind, "Suddenly, a sound from heaven like the roaring of a mighty windstorm" (Acts 2:2, NLT). A symbol of power, _____ , and movement. (2) _____ , "What looked like flames or tongues of fire appeared and sat on each of them" (Acts 2:3, NLT). A symbol of _____ , (3) _____ . "Everyone...began speaking in other languages" (Acts 2:4, NLT). Symbol of unity.

5. _____ . "Everyone present was filled with the Holy Spirit" (Acts 2:4, NLT). _____ of Holy Spirit.

6. _____ of Revival. "God pouring His presence on His people." (1) Old Testament illustration, Shekinah glory filling the temple. (2) Servants: Joshua (Numbers 27:18), Othniel (Judges 3:10), Gideon (Judges 6:24).

7. Today's definition of revival: (1) An _____ pouring out of God. (2) The sense of God's presence is _____ . (3) Believers give themselves to prayer, extended fellowship, testifying, and worship. (4) Significant ministry in the local church and _____ . (5) Believers make _____ and yield to spiritual growth. (6) New directions of ministry and church growth in numbers and ministry.

8. _____ . (1) Effective believers and (2) expanding churches.

B. Results of Revival

1. Great _____ of sin. "Peter's words pierced their hearts" (Acts 2:37, NLT).

2. Growing _____ . "Added to the church that day—about 3,000 in all" (Acts 2:41, NLT).

3. Effective _____ . "All the people had regard for them...more and more people believed and were brought to the Lord—crowds of both men and women" (Acts 5:13-14, NLT).

4. _____ of believers. "All believers met together...shared everything...shared their money with those in need. They worshiped together...shared their meals...enjoying the goodwill of all" (Acts 2:44-47, NLT).

5. Expanding _____ . "Many of them which heard the word believed; and the number of the men was about five thousand" (Acts 4:4, KJV).

6. Positive _____ . "They departed from the presence of the council rejoicing they were counted worthy to suffer" (Acts 5:41, KJV).

C. Biblical Attendance Records

1. _____ . "Those who believed...were baptized and added to the church that day—about 3,000 in all" (Acts 2:41, NLT).

2. _____ . "But many of the people who heard their message believed it, so the number of men who believed now totaled about 5,000" (Acts 4:4, NLT).

3. Saturation evangelism, reaching every _____ . "We gave you strict orders never again to teach in this man's name!" he said. "Instead, you have filled all Jerusalem with your teaching about him, and you want to make us responsible for his death!" (Acts 5:28, NLT).

4. _____ . "So God's message continued to spread. The number of believers greatly increased in Jerusalem, and many of the Jewish priests were converted, too" (Acts 6:7, NLT).

5. _____ . "The churches...were walking in the fear of the Lord, and...were multiplied" (Acts 9:31, KJV).

Fasting for Revival

"That is why the Lord says, 'turn to me now, while there is time. Give me your hearts. Come with fasting, weeping, and mourning. Don't tear your clothing in your grief, but tear your hearts instead.' Return to the Lord your God, for he is merciful and compassionate, slow to get angry and filled with unfailing love. He is eager to relent and not punish ...then, after doing all those things, I [the LORD] will pour out my Spirit upon all people. Your sons and daughters will prophesy. Your old men will dream dreams, and your young men will see visions. In those days I will pour out my Spirit even on servants—men and women alike."

Joel 2:12-13, 28-29, NLT

A. Preparing for Revival

1. Thomas Road Baptist Church has a wonderful past—great days of evangelism, and revival.

   a. Broke attendance records.

   b. Evangelistic crusades with hundreds saved, dozens baptized.

   c. Door-to-door evangelism. "And every day…house to house, they continued to teach and preach this message, 'Jesus is the Messiah.'"

   d. Baptism records.

2. Door-to-door doesn't seem to work in the United States as in the past, neither do big evangelistic meetings.

   Methods are many,

   Principles are few,

   Methods may change,

   But principles never do.

3. What still works:

   a. You telling others that God saved you, i.e., witnessing.

   b. Group prayer meetings and personal intercession.

   c. You faithfully serving God in your home, living godly, doing good deeds to others, attending, and serving in your church.

B. What Is Revival?

"Will You not revive us again, that Your people may rejoice in You?"
Psalm 85:6, NKJV

1. "Oh Lord, revive Your work in the midst of the years" (Habakkuk 3:2, NKJV).

2. What does revival _____ ? God pouring Himself on His people. "I will pour out My Spirit on all flesh" (Joel 2:28, NKJV).

3. What does revival _____ ? "That times of refreshing may come from the presence of the Lord" (Acts 3:19).

4. _____ definition: Restoration to life, i.e., consciousness, vigor, strength.

5. Christian definition: Return to New Testament life.

6. Your definition: Return to your _____ to Christ after conversion, and the _____ .

C. What Revival Is Not

1. Not a church or evangelistic _____ .

2. Not a church _____ .

3. Not your personal _____ or feelings.

D. Thomas Road Baptist Church Definition of Revival

God begins His work in our hearts where we repent of sin and poor testimony, renew our love to Christ, recommit ourselves to godly living, and meaningful ministry—usually accompanied with prayer, witnessing, and renewed dedication to God.

E. Some Characteristics of Revival

1. Can be an individual or group (church or Christian college).

2. Can be spontaneous from God or you can _____ it.

3. Can involve a family, or _____ , or area or denomination.

F. What Can You Do to Begin Revival?

1. _____ an imaginary circle on floor, ask God to begin a revival in that circle. Then step in and yield to do what God tells you.

2. _____ time of prayer and Bible reading.

3. _____ . Thomas Road Baptist Church and Liberty University called for a one day (24 hour) fast from sundown to sundown, which is called Yom Kippur Fast. "On the seventh month, on the tenth day (Yom Kippur) you shall go without eating" (Leviticus 16:29).

4. Joint _____ from sundown on Sunday to sundown on Monday.

5. Individuals may fast for longer time (3, 7, 21, or 40 days).

6. In the revival days of Spurgeon's ministry in England, a group of people called _____ would gather in the basement of the church under the pulpit. They would pray during each sermon. The only other church I know that did this was John Maxwell in his rapid growth days.

Igniters of Revival Lesson 3

Revival: 4 Plus 3

A. Revival When the Fire Fell

1. Solomon, _____ king. "I have
    become king in my father's [David] place" (2
    Chronicles 6:10, NLT).

2. _____ . "Then Solomon stood before
    the altar of the Lord in front of the entire community of
    Israel, and he lifted his hands in prayer" (2 Chronicles
    6:12).

3. _____ . "When Solomon finished
    praying, fire flashed down from heaven and burnt up
    the offering" (2 Chronicles 7:1).

4. _____ . "The glorious presence of
    the Lord filled the temple" (2 Chronicles 7:1).

5. _____ . "All the people...fell down in the ground and worshiped and praised the Lord" (2 Chronicles 7:3).

6. God's _____ to people enjoying God's fullness. "If my people who are called by my name will humble themselves and pray and seek my face and turn from their wicked ways, I will hear from heaven and will forgive their sins and restore their land" (2 Chronicles 7:14).

B. The Principles of 4 + 3 = 7 (Perfection)

1. Four things we must do to _____
   God's presence:

   a. _____ . "God opposes the proud,
      but favors the humble. Humble yourselves before
      God" (James 4:6-7, NLT).

   b. Pray, recognize your _____ ,
      confess it to God,
      _____ God to answer, and
      _____ the problem.

   c. Seek. Give all your _____ to God,
      give the first of your time, give your energy to serve
      God, _____ your time, talents,
      and tithes to God.

   d. Turn from your wicked ways
      , _____ anything between
      you and God, _____ what sin
      possess you. _____ it to God, ask
      for _____ . "If we confess our sins
      to him, he is faithful and just to forgive us our sins
      and to cleanse us from all wickedness" (1 John 1:9,
      NLT).

2. Three things God will do for you:

   a. _____ . Your confession will get God's attention. "It's your sins that have cut you off from God. Because of your sins, he has turned away and will not listen anymore" (Isaiah 59:2, NLT).

   b. _____ their sins. First, _____ cleanse our sins recorded in God's book. Second, the actual _____ of sin in our lives, and the _____ of sin over our lives, i.e., slavery to sin (Romans 7).

   c. _____ their land. In the Old Testament, Israel lost the Promised Land because of idols. In the New Testament it means _____ , new life, new desires to live and serve. _____ , "This means that anyone who belongs to Christ has become a new person. The old life is gone; a new life has begun!" (2 Corinthians 5:17, NLT).

c. Practical Steps to Keep/Bring Revival

1. Study God's recent revivals. _____
   of Revival.

2. Invite "carriers of revival" to testify their experience in a revival.

3. Call for _____
   for revival in our church and in private intercession.

4. _____ on the conditions that lead
   to revival.

5. Give people the _____ to make a
   deeper commitment to revival (sign a pledge to pray,
   come and pray at altar, call for prayer groups, etc.).

6. Give people opportunity to _____
   of God's work in their life (in public meetings, by video,
   etc.).

7. Spread the revival—use every
   available _____ , to challenge every
   available _____ , at every available
   _____ , to be involved in every
   available way.

Teacher's Outlines

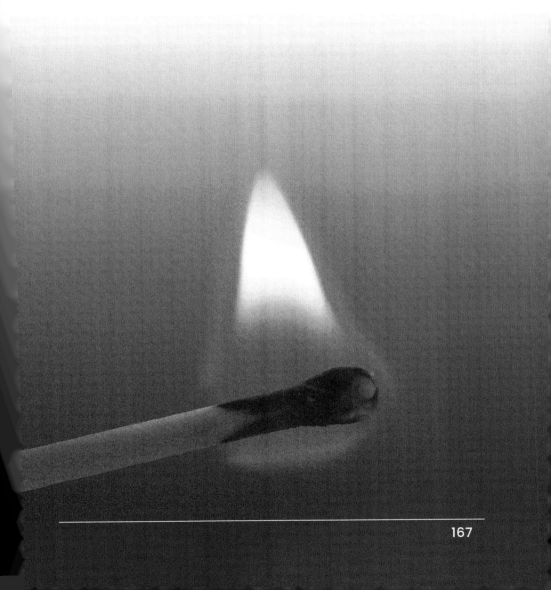

Igniters of Revival Lesson 1

A Revived Church

"Those who believed what Peter said were baptized and added to the church that day—about 3,000 in all. All the believers devoted themselves to the apostles' teaching, and to fellowship, and to sharing in meals (including the Lord's Supper), and to prayer. A deep sense of awe came over them all, and the apostles performed many miraculous signs and wonders. And all the believers met together in one place and shared everything they had ...all the while praising God and enjoying the goodwill of all the people. And each day the Lord added to their fellowship those who were being saved."

Acts 2:41-45, 47, NLT

A. First Church Began with Revival

1. <u>What is revival</u>? "I will pour out my Spirit upon all people" (Joel 2:28, NLT).

2. <u>Preparation</u>. "Do not leave Jerusalem until the Father sends you the gift he promised" (Acts 1:4, NLT). "They all met together and were constantly united in prayer" (Acts 1:14, NLT).

3. <u>Unity</u>. "All the believers were meeting together in one place" (Acts 2:1, NLT).

4. <u>Three signs</u>: (1) Wind, "Suddenly, a sound from heaven like the roaring of a mighty windstorm" (Acts 2:2, NLT). A symbol of power, <u>life</u>, and movement. (2) <u>Fire</u>, "What looked like flames or tongues of fire appeared and sat on each of them" (Acts 2:3, NLT). A symbol of <u>purity</u>, (3) <u>Tongues</u>. "Everyone...began speaking in other languages" (Acts 2:4, NLT). Symbol of unity.

5. <u>Power</u>. "Everyone present was filled with the Holy Spirit" (Acts 2:4, NLT). <u>Baptized</u> of Holy Spirit.

6. <u>Description</u> of Revival. "God pouring His presence on His people." (1) Old Testament illustration, Shekinah glory filling the temple. (2) Servants: Joshua (Numbers 27:18), Othniel (Judges 3:10), Gideon (Judges 6:24).

7. Today's definition of revival: (1) An <u>extraordinary</u> pouring out of God. (2) The sense of God's presence is <u>experienced</u>. (3) Believers give themselves to prayer, extended fellowship, testifying, and worship. (4) Significant ministry in the local church and <u>evangelistic outreach</u>. (5) Believers make <u>personal sacrifices</u> and yield to spiritual growth. (6) New directions of ministry and church growth in numbers and ministry.

8. <u>Produces</u>. (1) Effective believers and (2) expanding churches.

B. Results of Revival

1. Great <u>conviction</u> of sin. "Peter's words pierced their hearts" (Acts 2:37, NLT).

2. Growing <u>results</u>. "Added to the church that day—about 3,000 in all" (Acts 2:41, NLT).

3. Effective <u>testimony</u>. "All the people had regard for them...more and more people believed and were brought to the Lord—crowds of both men and women" (Acts 5:13-14, NLT).

4. Harmony/unity of believers. "All believers met together...shared everything...shared their money with those in need. They worshiped together...shared their meals...enjoying the good will of all" (Acts 2:44-47, NLT).

5. Expanding influence. "Many of them which heard the word believed; and the number of the men was about five thousand" (Acts 4:4, KJV).

6. Positive response. "They departed from the presence of the council rejoicing they were counted worthy to suffer" (Acts 5:41, KJV).

C. Biblical Attendance Records

1. Pentecost. "Those who believed...were baptized and added to the church that day—about 3,000 in all" (Acts 2:41, NLT).

2. Families Added. "But many of the people who heard their message believed it, so the number of men who believed now totaled about 5,000" (Acts 4:4, NLT).

3. Saturation evangelism, reaching every <u>available person</u>. "We gave you strict orders never again to teach in this man's name!" he said. "Instead, you have filled all Jerusalem with your teaching about him, and you want to make us responsible for his death!" (Acts 5:28, NLT).

4. <u>More than could be counted</u>. "So God's message continued to spread. The number of believers greatly increased in Jerusalem, and many of the Jewish priests were converted, too" (Acts 6:7, NLT).

5. <u>Churches multiply</u>. "The churches...were walking in the fear of the Lord, and...were multiplied" (Acts 9:31, KJV).

Fasting for Revival

"That is why the Lord says, 'turn to me now, while there is time. Give me your hearts. Come with fasting, weeping, and mourning. Don't tear your clothing in your grief, but tear your hearts instead.' Return to the Lord your God, for he is merciful and compassionate, slow to get angry and filled with unfailing love. He is eager to relent and not punish ...then, after doing all those things, I [the LORD] will pour out my Spirit upon all people. Your sons and daughters will prophesy. Your old men will dream dreams, and your young men will see visions. In those days I will pour out my Spirit even on servants—men and women alike."

Joel 2:12-13, 28-29, NLT

A. Preparing for Revival

1. Thomas Road Baptist Church has a wonderful past—great days of evangelism, and revival.

   a. Broke attendance records.

   b. Evangelistic crusades with hundreds saved, dozens baptized.

   c. Door-to-door evangelism. "And every day...house to house, they continued to teach and preach this message, 'Jesus is the Messiah.'"

   d. Baptism records.

2. Door-to-door doesn't seem to work in the United States as in the past, neither do big evangelistic meetings.

   Methods are many,
   Principles are few,
   Methods may change,
   But principles never do.

3. What still works:

    a. You telling others that God saved you, i.e., witnessing.

    b. Group prayer meetings and personal intercession.

    c. You faithfully serving God in your home, living godly, doing good deeds to others, attending, and serving in your church.

B. What Is Revival?

"Will You not revive us again, that Your people may rejoice in You?"
Psalm 85:6, NKJV

1. "Oh Lord, revive Your work in the midst of the years" (Habakkuk 3:2, NKJV).

2. What does revival <u>look like</u>? God pouring Himself on His people. "I will pour out My Spirit on all flesh" (Joel 2:28, NKJV).

3. What does revival <u>do</u>? "That times of refreshing may come from the presence of the Lord" (Acts 3:19).

4. <u>Dictionary</u> definition: Restoration to life, i.e., consciousness, vigor, strength.

5. Christian definition: Return to New Testament life.

6. Your definition: Return to your <u>original commitment</u> to Christ after conversion, and the <u>joy of your salvation</u>.

C. What Revival Is Not

1. Not a church or evangelistic <u>crusade</u>.

2. Not a church <u>meeting</u>.

3. Not your personal <u>excitement</u> or feelings.

D. Thomas Road Baptist Church Definition of Revival

God begins His work in our hearts where we repent of sin and poor testimony, renew our love to Christ, recommit ourselves to godly living, and meaningful ministry—usually accompanied with prayer, witnessing, and renewed dedication to God.

E. Some Characteristics of Revival

1. Can be an individual or group (church or Christian college).

2. Can be spontaneous from God or you can <u>initiate</u> it.

3. Can involve a family, or <u>total church</u>, or area or denomination.

F. What Can You Do to Begin Revival?

1. <u>Draw</u> an imaginary circle on floor, ask God to begin a revival in that circle. Then step in and yield to do what God tells you.

2. <u>Extended</u> time of prayer and Bible reading.

3. <u>Fast</u>. Thomas Road Baptist Church and Liberty University called for a one day (24 hour) fast from sundown to sundown, which is called Yom Kippur Fast. "On the seventh month, on the tenth day (Yom Kippur) you shall go without eating" (Leviticus 16:29, AV).

4. Joint <u>church fast</u> from sundown on Sunday to sundown on Monday.

5. Individuals may fast for longer time (3, 7, 21, or 40 days).

6. In the revival days of Spurgeon's ministry in England, a group of people called <u>watchers</u> would gather in the basement of the church under the pulpit. They would pray during each sermon. The only other church I know that did this was John Maxwell in his rapid growth days.

Igniters of Revival Lesson 3

Revival: 4 Plus 3

A. Revival When the Fire Fell

1. Solomon, <u>new</u> king. "I have become king in my father's [David] place" (2 Chronicles 6:10, NLT).

2. <u>Right place</u>. "Then Solomon stood before the altar of the Lord in front of the entire community of Israel, and he lifted his hands in prayer" (2 Chronicles 6:12).

3. <u>Revival fire</u>. "When Solomon finished praying, fire flashed down from heaven and burnt up the offering" (2 Chronicles 7:1).

4. <u>God showed up</u>. "The glorious presence of the Lord filled the Temple" (2 Chronicles 7:1).

5. <u>Response</u>. "All the people...fell down in the ground and worshiped and praised the Lord" (2 Chronicles 7:3).

6. God's <u>warning/reminder</u> to people enjoying God's fullness. "If my people who are called by my name will humble themselves and pray and seek my face and turn from their wicked ways, I will hear from heaven and will forgive their sins and restore their land" (2 Chronicles 7:14).

B. The Principles of 4 + 3 = 7 (Perfection)

1. Four things we must do to <u>keep/regain</u> God's presence:

   a. <u>Humble</u>. "God opposes the proud, but favors the humble. Humble yourselves before God" (James 4:6–7, NLT).

   b. Pray, recognize your <u>need</u>, confess it to God, <u>ask</u> God to answer, and <u>fix</u> the problem.

   c. Seek. Give all your <u>attention</u> to God, give the first of your time, give your energy to serve God, <u>dedicate</u> your time, talents, and tithes to God.

   d. Turn from your wicked ways, <u>identify</u> anything between you and God, <u>confess</u> what sin possess you. <u>Surrender</u> it to God, ask for <u>cleansing</u>. "If we confess our sins to him, he is faithful and just to forgive us our sins and to cleanse us from all wickedness" (1 John 1:9, NLT).

2. Three things God will do for you:

   a. <u>Hear</u>. Your confession will get God's attention. "It's your sins that have cut you off from God. Because of your sins, he has turned away and will not listen anymore" (Isaiah 59:2, NLT).

   b. <u>Forgive</u> their sins. First, <u>judicial</u> cleanse our sins recorded in God's book. Second, the actual <u>presence</u> of sin in our lives, and the <u>control</u> of sin over our lives, i.e., slavery to sin (Romans 7).

   c. <u>Restore</u> their land. In the Old Testament, Israel lost the Promised Land because of idols. In the New Testament it means <u>regeneration</u>, new life, new desires to live and serve. <u>Transformation</u>, "This means that anyone who belongs to Christ has become a new person. The old life is gone; a new life has begun!" (2 Corinthians 5:17, NLT).

c. Practical Steps to Keep/Bring Revival

1. Study God's recent revivals. <u>Igniters</u> of Revival.

2. Invite "carriers of revival" to testify their experience in a revival.

3. Call for <u>individual and corporate prayer</u> for revival in our church and in private intercession.

4. <u>Preach</u> on the conditions that lead to revival.

5. Give people the <u>opportunity</u> to make a deeper commitment to revival (sign a pledge to pray, come and pray at altar, call for prayer groups, etc.).

6. Give people opportunity to <u>testify</u> of God's work in their life (in public meetings, by video, etc.).

7. Spread the revival—use every available <u>means</u>, to challenge every available <u>person</u>, at every available <u>time</u>, to be involved in every available way.

Notes

Notes

About

Dr. Elmer L. Towns

Dr. Elmer Towns is Dean Emeritus of the School of Religion and Theological Seminary at Liberty University, which he cofounded in 1977. He published more than 100 books, several accepted as college textbooks. He is a recipient of the Gold Medallion Award awarded by the Christian Booksellers Association. He holds a visiting professorship rank at five seminaries, and received six honorary doctoral degrees. He earned a B.S. from Northwestern College, a M.A. from Southern Methodist University, a Th.M. from Dallas Theological Seminary, a MRE from Garrett Theological Seminary, and a D.Min. from Fuller Theological Seminary.

Made in the USA
Middletown, DE
17 September 2022